ADVENTUROUS PREACHING

ADVENTUROUS PREACHING

THE LYMAN BEECHER LECTURES AT YALE

JAMES H. ROBINSON

CHANNEL PRESS, GREAT NECK, NEW YORK

THIS BOOK IS AFFECTIONATELY DEDICATED TO THE SEMINARY STUDENTS WITH WHOM I HAVE WORKED. ASSISTING THEIR PRACTICAL PREPARATION FOR THE GOSPEL MINISTRY HAS BEEN MY MOST REWARDING ASSOCIATION; THEIR LIVES HAVE GREATLY ENRICHED MY OWN; THEIR WORK FOR THE KINGDOM IN MANY PARTS OF THE WORLD HAS HELPED BRING IT A LITTLE NEARER.

ACKNOWLEDGMENT

I WANT to express my sincere appreciation to Dean Liston Pope and the faculty of Yale Divinity School for inviting me to give the 1955 Lyman Beecher lectures; to the officers and members of the Church of the Master, who graciously gave me the time away from my duties to prepare the manuscript; to the Rev. Leonard Seibert Jones of Covina, California, and Dr. Glenn McGee of Trinity Presbyterian Church in Tuscon, Arizona, for their kindness in providing a quiet retreat where I could work; to Mrs. Boyd V. McDougall of Tucson, Arizona, for her untiring efforts and advice in the preparation of the manuscript; and to my office staff for all the tedious and laborious details they undertook on my behalf beyond their assigned duties.

Biblical quotations are from the *King James Version*, except for the passages in Chapter One, pages 24–25, and in Chapter Six, page 161, which are from the *Revised Standard Version*, copyright, 1946, 1952, by the Division of Christian Education of the National Council of the Churches of Christ in the U.S.A.

I also wish to thank the following publishers for permission to quote from their copyrighted works:

HARPER AND BROTHERS (Elton Trueblood, *The Predicament of Modern Man;* Gerald Kennedy, *With Singleness of Heart;* Henry Sloane Coffin, *What to Preach;* Walter Horton, *Can*

Christianity Save Civilization; Paul Scherer, *The Plight of Freedom*)

ABINGDON PRESS (Murray H. Leiffer, *The Effective City Church;* Leslie Weatherhead, *The Significance of Silence;* Seward Hiltner, *Pastoral Counseling*)

CHARLES SCRIBNER'S SONS (Charles Lindbergh, *Of Flight and Life;* Paul Tillich, *Shaking of the Foundations*)

ASSOCIATION PRESS (Charles Kean, *Christianity and the Cultural Crisis*)

HARCOURT, BRACE AND COMPANY (Karl Stern, *The Third Revolution*)

HENRY HOLT AND COMPANY (Frances G. Wickes, *The Inner Life Man*)

OXFORD UNIVERSITY PRESS (Arnold Toynbee, *The World and the West*)

PANTHEON BOOKS (Anne Morrow Lindbergh, *Gift from the Sea*)

SIMON AND SCHUSTER (Joshua Loth Liebman, *Peace of Mind*)

VIKING PRESS (James Weldon Johnson, *God's Trombones*)

The City Church ("Mortar and Morals," by David Barry, October 27, 1954, issue)

The Reporter ("Going Down This Street, Lord," by William Harlan Hale, January 13, 1955, issue)

And a special thanks to Mr. Robinson Jeffers for permission to quote from his poem, "Shine, Perishing Republic."

TABLE OF CONTENTS

PREFACE

JAMES ROBINSON'S Lyman Beecher lectures on preaching cannot be fully appreciated without knowing something more about the author than the lectures reveal, however lucid they are in presenting the essential message of a very remarkable young man—a minister, incidentally, who is probably more youthful than anyone previously called to give the Lyman Beecher lectures. The reason this explanation is necessary is that the message of the gospel has probably never been more wrought by a process of "blood, sweat and tears" than his message. No contemporary preacher has a more interesting biographical background for his message than James Robinson.

Dr. Robinson is a very successful Negro minister, and the first Negro to be invited to give the Beecher lectures. But that is not his chief or only claim to uniqueness. In order to explain the significance of the man and his message, it is necessary to refer to James Robinson's autobiography, which was published in 1950. Entitled *Road Without Turning*, this very honest and revealing life-story pictures the spiritual background of these lectures with great clarity. James Robinson was born in the abject poverty of a Negro home, the son of a father who was passionately religious after the manner of the pentecostal sectarianism, which represents such a religious force, particularly among Negroes. His mother, on the other hand, while of religious temperament, was skeptical of her husband's religion. It

11

would be interesting to speculate in what way these two influences contributed to the religious development of their son, though it is obvious that James' passion for an education, pursued with a singleminded and tough resolution, was derived chiefly from the mother. The young man, after the death of his mother, was taken care of by various relatives who exhibited the mutuality of a larger family, one of the graces of the life of the very poor.

The resourcefulness, tenacity, and—occasionally—guile with which the young man set out to acquire an education in high school, college, and seminary is itself an interesting story, but does not contribute directly to insight into the genius of the preacher except to suggest various earnests of the kind of resourcefulness which entered into the success of his ministry.

What is more important for our understanding is his frank revelation of the way he became obsessed, as any intelligent and sensitive young Negro must, with the fact and the problem of the white man's injustice to the Negro people. His life reveals the truth of the contention of a great law professor, Dr. Edmund Cahn, that the sense of injustice is the most vivid expression of the sense of justice, a thesis which is vividly exemplified in the life and teachings of the Hebrew prophets. But the animus against the white man was so strong in young Robinson's life that it required time and experience and the wisdom of the gospel to fit the reaction to injustice, which inspired it to be incorporated into his Christian ministry. That is a part of the engaging story of James Robinson.

Robinson went from the seminary to the church which he still serves, though the world has become his parish. In that church he set about immediately to combine the preaching of the gospel with every kind of service to his hard-pressed people. He became a leader in what is usually called "social service," and which includes concern for the whole man with all his ills and perplexities, physical, psychological, and social. In the pursuit of these aims he became one of the founders of an interracial hospital in New York. Incidentally, he had one flyer in politics, when the Liberal party in a recent campaign nominated him for the position of Borough President of Manhattan. He was defeated; but his nomination persuaded the Democratic party also to nominate their first Negro to the same position, and this candidate was elected and still serves.

As if the double ministry were not enough, Robinson has recently been called to be active on the world scene. He participated in a world trip of a commission to examine the color problem in the Asian and African world, and to bear testimony to the resources of American democracy to work for solutions of the racial injustice which represents the "American dilemma," and which Communist propaganda uses consistently against the prestige of the West.

More recently, at the request of several organizations, he again went to Africa to make further investigations. As a Negro he had both a perspective on the issues and a source of information which no previous investigator could have. His report upon his mission proved that the young minister had acquired not only the grace of the gospel, but the wisdom of Christian statesmanship.

These lectures proceed, in other words, from the experience of a singularly rich and fruitful ministry. The words of this volume are weighty enough, but they will become more weighty if the reader recognizes the significance of the life and ministry from which they have been wrought. It is safe to say that the American church can boast of no more creative preaching of the Word than that which James Robinson has practiced at the Church of the Master in New York.

While these Beecher lectures have a special appeal because of the unique history and experience of the author, they would be memorable in any event because they deal not only with the message of the preacher but with the whole strategy of the church, in the city, in suburbia, and on the mission field. They also consistently insist on the social relevance of the gospel message without obscuring the heart of the evangelical message. They therefore present us with the best in the "social gospel" tradition and relate it creatively to the total evangelical message of the church. They reveal that the author is a church statesman of the first order whose message is of importance partly because of, and partly despite, the unique history and experience which give his words wings.

REINHOLD NIEBUHR

ADVENTUROUS PREACHING

THE PREACHER
UNDER JUDGMENT

SITUATIONS of life are constantly in flux. We are moved into greater dimensions by the inexorable march of scientific advancement; at the same time, new knowledge makes the globe shrink small. Yet at the heart and core of all things, both those which enlarge and those which diminish our world, is man—man, "the temple of the living"—and everything else must be seen in proportion to him.

Man is a being of God. Man is a psychological reality. He must relate himself—or be related—to God, to other men, to his past, and to the powerful new resources at his command. The whole meaning of his life must be evaluated and interpreted.

And this mighty task of interpretation and evaluation is a religious problem. The minister is not just a part of it; he is the heart of it.

We need every reminder we can find to help us understand the holiness of our ministry. We are stewards of the mysteries of God. We are set apart by His grace, not *from* people, but rather *among* them.

There is a world of difference between these two concepts: the Christian religion can never be considered apart from life, but always as a part of every aspect of existence, as a part of that grand design of God "in Whom we live and move and have our being." And this is most vitally true in times of economic, social, scientific, and political change.

Under the impact of modern forces in our society, the concept of the ministry has changed, and is still changing. The holy fellowship with God, the foundation of the unique human relationship in history—that of the pastor and his people—is being continually reduced to a professional level. In place of the holiness of the call, vocational aptitude tests are sometimes substituted. Modern testing methods may have validity, but they are no adequate replacement for the intense personal relationship between a minister and his God. They are no substitute for that judgment which is implied by the call and the will of God.

"How often does the minister make the sermon page of the daily paper?" "Is he popular?" "Can he speak well?" Such questions often take precedence over the most important one: "Does he have anything to say?"

The call of God is not a one-way street to bigger and better pulpits. The call of God often compels His ablest and most seasoned veterans to labor where the salients of evil are deeply entrenched and where the secular rewards are few. But surely God is as wise in the deployment of His forces to win eternal victories as is a sales executive to increase his profits or a general to win a battle!

It is undoubtedly proper for people in the secular professions to make advancement to bigger and better posts the criterion of worth. But God has not called us to preach as though preaching were but a waystop on the highway to riches, renown, and recognition. He has called us, instead, to the service of His Kingdom and the leadership of men and women who seek that Kingdom.

In this service, it is all too easy for us to hurl anathemas against the sins of men and the evils of society—and do it without recognizing our own complicity as sinners under judgment. The High Priest, in Old Testament days, knew that he was under the judgment of God. When he went into the Holy of Holies on the Day of Atonement, he confessed his own sins as he proceeded to confess for all the people. "All men have sinned and fallen short of the glory of God." Today as then, "all men" is a phrase which includes the minister.

The best that he can be is a redeemed sinner. It is only through the minister's recognition of this need for forgiveness and divine assistance that he is compassionate enough to lead the people. When a clergyman does not relate to the needs of people in warm, personal terms, it is usually the result of beating too straight a path from the retreat of the study to the safe vantage point of the pulpit. Or, in these days of increased specialization in a world which strives to be coldly mechanical and efficient—it is a result of the detachment of particularism.

Every pastor knows the anguish of trying to make the material which specialists send him relevant to the needs and problems of his own congregation. It is usually a most disheartening task. Indeed, I have frequently felt that specialists in the field of religion ought to have regular sabbaticals—that they should be freed to return to the local scene in order to test their theories. At the very least, they should get to read to *people* what they have written for pastors to use. Goodness knows that an advanced society like ours demands trained specialists in religious work, as in every other phase of life, but preachers must never lose contact with the main stream of the Church of Christ. They must never lose contact with people.

The preacher once enjoyed a wide and uniquely central place in the life of our society. Time and progress have changed it radically. The place is still unique, but it is no longer central. There was a time in our country when the minister played a profoundly significant role in shaping government, laying the foundations of education, organizing and administering schools and colleges, hospitals and welfare societies. He was more than a community or civic leader. He was the *cornerstone* of the community.

He helped to write the laws, establish the rules of conduct. He became the first social worker and counselor. So much flowed about him that his advice and judgment were sought on every conceivable matter.

When Henry Ward Beecher initiated the Lyman Beecher lectures, he was a partner in several businesses, an editor, a columnist, and a politician, both at the grass-roots and Presidential levels. In addition to seeking him out for pastoral advice, people came to his house as early as six each morning for advice on financial, civic, and business matters. His endorsement of products was sought as avidly as is the endorsement of a movie idol or baseball star today.

Within my own lifetime, and particularly among the Negro clergy, I have seen a complete change take place. This change occurred more slowly among Negroes because of the peculiarities of the race problem; and so even as recently as twenty-five years ago, the Negro preacher held an undisputed position of prestige and effectiveness in the land, admired and looked to for leadership of his people by whites and Negroes alike. Today, like other clergymen, he is no longer a lord of life and action. (Many American politicians of both parties have been less aware of this change, incidentally, than the average Negro Christian. As late as the last Presidential election, politicians of one party thought that by securing the endorsement of some Negro clergymen they could swing the whole Negro vote.)

The Negro minister is destined to continue to lose ground and influence. Fewer than a hundred seminary-trained Negro ministers graduate from all the seminaries of this country annually. This means that only one-seventh of the number needed each year are educated clergymen. Yet at the very same time, over twenty thousand Negroes graduate from colleges and universities each year, and well over a thousand annually receive graduate degrees. It is obvious that few of this group, if any, will be content to relate to churches led by untrained ministers.[1]

A host of abler and more skillfully trained professionals now perform many of the functions which the minister once carried out. It is no discredit to the preacher that the new professionals are the products of an increasingly complex society, and that they do a better job in the realm of their specialty than the minister. It is both natural and right that they should, because they are trained to the highly skilled specializations demanded by our society. We can be grateful to God that there are others to help carry the burden when social, human, economic, and religious problems outrun the happiness and security which God meant for His children to have. The preacher can have more time today to devote himself to the special task to which God has called him. Sooner than later, even the specialist will seek the minister either for help on the moral problem of his own life, or for cooperation on the larger moral problems of society.

Unhappily, the change has been accompanied by a secularization of life. This secularization has by its very nature, and by the efforts of many of the new professionals, sought to isolate the preacher and drive him even farther into the background. One example will suffice.

Social work, which ought to be the handmaiden of the church —since both deal with the problem of relating man wholesomely to his environment—has developed largely outside the sphere of religious influence. Its dictum often is "change the environment and you change the man." An old Baptist deacon sat in a city council meeting listening to a sociologist plead for an increased appropriation for welfare and low-cost housing projects. The statistics-laden appeal was based on the assumption that the answer to anti-social attitudes, crime, broken homes, and delinquency lay mainly in changing the conditions under which people live. The deacon made an adequate and telling reply when he said, "I believe in more taxes to discharge our duty to the less fortunate, and also in more low-cost housing, but this isn't enough. We need some good religion to help make a new people for the new clothes and the new houses, for when you bring both of these together then you've got a far more lasting answer to human needs."

It is only fair to admit that many clergymen have not kept pace with progress and advancement. The result is that we are increasingly isolated within the cloisters of the church. We begin to resemble appendages to our society. The nation rushes by, and we draw solace from the fact that as they pass they tip their hats in a hurried, vestigial gesture of respect.

When we are not by-passed altogether, we are invited with misgiving and skepticism to lend the blessing of God to all manner of social gatherings; and the hope is plainly evident to all but the most insensitive that we will not stay at the function long enough to become a kill-joy. We are invited to decorate banquet tables as a token-fetish which represents some vague necessity of propitiating the deity; or we are tolerated because we are believed to bring respectability to assorted assemblages of labor unions, political parties, patriotic rallies, and sundry gatherings, which then proceed to go their own way without further reference to the judgment of God.

Of course, in times of tragedy and calamity, when men reach their extremities, we are most welcome, and eagerly kept close at hand until the crisis is past. It is not even uncommon in these days for church members to reserve a special niche for the preacher, or a special deference which is called *respect;* even this is often merely a technique to keep us at arm's length until urgency demands the undergirding of "the everlasting arms."

But that is not all. In this day of scientific investigation, progressive education, and trust in the sentimental goodness of men, we who are ministers hear people tell us over and over that they do not want to be "preached to." They want us merely to hold a "discussion group" with them.

The result has been that some of us feel the tragic impotence of our preaching, and not infrequently ask ourselves, "Is it worth anything?" Every minister knows the agonizing frustration which Victor Hugo expressed so well in the last stanza of his poem, *The Age Is Great and Strong:*

> But in this boasted arch of wrong and error,
> 'Mid the vast splendor of an age that glows,
> One thing, O Jesus, fills my heart with terror:
> The echo of thy voice still feebler grows.

In an effort to catch up with the galloping changes in our troubled society and to become more acceptable, we have learned some of the lessons of the secular world all too well, and have adopted too many of its codes. The city doctor seldom responds to an urgent midnight call any more; we ministers try to reduce the extreme circumstances of men and women to office hours. The psychologist enjoins us to establish empathy with our parishioners, but never to become too identified with their troubles and their sorrows. The caseworker reduces home visits to a minimum in the interest of a larger caseload, and we likewise curtail our visiting, but in what interest I am not so sure. Some lawyers make their living by helping clients short-change the law, but we also engage in short-changing when we fail to hold up the high moral demands of righteousness and the inevitable consequences of wrong actions.

All professionals create as wide a gap as possible between their homes and their work. I doubt seriously that this separation of the preacher's home from his work is a reliable mark of progress and religious growth, for it prevents his home from being the center of a great Christian influence.

When I was in Union Seminary, a few clergymen tried to start a labor union to look out for the rights and privileges of preachers, as though reliance on the Lord God, whose messengers we claim to be, were not sufficient for our protection. Thank God, and to our eternal credit, they did not succeed.

The whole world seems to be trying to turn itself into a machine—a mechanical nightmare, empty of its human warmth and unaware of its potentially divine personal content and absolutely divine spiritual content. A good case is the rush hour twice a day on subways, street cars and buses, where men and women crush themselves together in an indecent proximity from which animals would instinctively withdraw. The tragedy is that we feel neither disgust with our society, which forces us to do this, nor shame with ourselves for our loss of human dignity. Man is in danger of becoming an unthinking machine. And at the same time, this machine wants somehow to involve the preacher as a cog in the demonic process . . . a cog which moves no gears, does no work, just spins aimlessly—as useless as reins on an automobile.

If he were a machine, man could be conveniently discarded when his usefulness was past. But man is a soul, a potentially divine image of God, of Whose life and spirit he partakes. I once saw a cartoon in the *New Yorker* showing a proud father as he looked through the hospital nursery window at his new-born son. The artist pictured the young man as he exclaimed to a friend, "It's a miracle." The cartoonist meant this to be a joke, because birth is so commonplace—but he never in his life said anything more true. Birth was and always will be a miracle because it is evidence of the continued creativity of God which has no end—a theism which all of us may understand. All life is still a miracle. The fact that we know all the processes of life does not in any degree detract from the essence of its miraculous qualities. We do not know how it began, and although we may destroy one phase of it, we cannot destroy the soul. Nor can we initiate the process of life. Life is a holy thing, for it is the extension of eternal God in the world. The preacher is under judgment to keep this concept always before our society, although society is rushing headlong to destroy it. Woe unto us if we abdicate our high calling and stand idly by!

We cannot rightly quarrel with the methods of other professionals because there are good reasons why they develop the way they do. Nevertheless, we may judge them. They have made a practical and expedient decision in terms of personal desires and abilities. Ours is infinitely larger. Ours is a divine call to a holy task. The work we do is holy, and the place from which we preach is a holy place—as holy as the spot where Moses stood when God called him. There is a great difference between our call and the vocation of doctor, lawyer, social worker; between our task and their professions. The distance is as great as that between the fall of Adam and the resurrection of Jesus.

Listen to the lofty definition of our call as St. Paul puts it:

> Therefore, having this ministry by the mercy of God, we do not lose heart. We have renounced disgraceful, underhanded ways; we refuse to practice cunning or to

tamper with God's word, but by the open statement of the truth, we would commend ourselves to every man's conscience in the sight of God. And even if our gospel is veiled, it is veiled only to those who are perishing. In their case the god of this world has blinded the minds of the unbelievers, to keep them from seeing the light of the gospel of the glory of Christ, who is the likeness of God. For what we preach is not ourselves, but Jesus Christ as Lord, with ourselves as your servants for Jesus' sake. For it is the God who said, "Let light shine out of darkness," who has shone in our hearts to give the light of the knowledge of the glory of God in the face of Christ. (II CORINTHIANS 4: 1–6)

When we preach to the congregation or to the nation, we are preaching to ourselves as well. We are windows through which God's light may shine on the world. "God using me to help Him," as George Eliot put it in her poem, *Stradivarius*. The minister is under the eternal compunction to be something more than a professional in a secularized society, for he carries "a treasure in earthen vessels that excellency of his work may be of God" and not of himself.

A number of powerful forces have spun our society through a torturous wringer and left it greatly wanting in basic security and happiness. The modern enlightenment wrought by scientific achievement has led to a false optimism about the ultimate goodness of man. The expectation of a brave new world brought about through technical prowess and universal education has sought to guide the destinies of men and nations with a humanism based upon reason. Millions lent their best efforts to the notion that human ability without God, but with a combination of technical achievement, scientific knowledge, economic reconstruction and the manipulation of men by psychological determinism, would find the proper stimuli for human action. Millions believed that a purely ethical consideration of individual and national conduct would be sufficient to bring about the good life, peace on earth, and the abundant society for all.

This pathetic faith in blind mechanical optimism, powerful as it is, has sustained a series of continuous shocks. Arrogant in our increased knowledge of material things, we have not had a corresponding growth in our knowledge of the love of God, nor have we properly harnessed our abilities to the creative and loving will of God. Man's sinful nature has been completely ignored by the new technology in which the world has put such trust. When the goal seems within our grasp, we find ourselves in a "race with catastrophe," the extent of which reveals that man has the power to turn what might have been a blessing into a curse.

It is little wonder that, under the influence of these powerful forces by which society has been changed, the preacher has lost much power and influence. People have failed to realize that man, though only a little lower than the angels, is still an animal in need of something to guide his spiritual life. They have failed to realize that humanism is not enough.

Despite advancement, progress, and change, the most important problem of our time is a spiritual problem. The shock of two world wars has rocked our faith in the supposed goodness of man and the inevitable unification of the world by science. But it did not shake it enough to jar us loose from all of our illusions. We were thrown back upon God by the exigencies of events. Even there we compromised, for God was reduced by the modern world to a vague equality with worldly power, scientific knowledge, and ethics. We did not argue about His presence. We just organized our lives to take in a more convenient concept. People ceased opposing religion; they did something worse. They began either to ignore it or to use it as a touchstone to success or as an escape from fear. Yet as a result, the preacher came back, at least in part, into his own.

Even Bertrand Russell, the materialist, humanist, realist, and, in one sense at least, idealist, now says, after years of wandering, "When all is said and done, it would be a pity if mankind turned out to be no more dignified than an ape playing with a box of matches in a petroleum dump."[2]

Although it does seem that way at times, man *is* a rational and

spiritual being. An ape would not know the Godlike potentialities which his folly jeopardized, but man knows the full extent
of the power he experiences and the moral responsibility which
evolves therefrom. At the point where man can discern between
the relative, the comparative, and the ultimate, and accept or re-
ject responsibility for wise and right use of increased scientific
knowledge, he has already entered the realm of the spiritual.
The future peace, security, and happiness of the world depends
more upon what men do to understand the spiritual motivation of
their lives, in relation to scientific and mechanical progress and
power, than upon how much they understand their new technological developments. The preacher is never isolated from this
problem, unless he allows himself to be.

God needs the voice of the preacher more than ever before;
and God's need is man's need, whether man knows it or not. In the
circle of eternity, man's baser instincts have been intertwined
since life began. But the time relation in the application of knowledge, reason, moral influence, and religious insight is only a few
degrees of the three hundred sixty degrees of the stuff with
which man began life. A wit put the problem with humorous can-
dor when he said, "The Darwinian man, though well behaved, is
only at best a monkey shaved." However, in a more serious vein,
it seems reasonable that man is in the graduate school of scientific
investigation and material achievement, but hardly out of the
kindergarten in the application of the spiritual to the material.
Modern man's egotism, ability, and pride, are merely overlaid with
a thin layer of culture.

The preacher has an important task assigned him by God. He is
to help men understand the relatively simple fact that the conditions which have been most conducive to scientific advance were
created by the Christian view of the world. Men create nothing
new; they merely discover what God has already done, or, as
someone has said, "think God's thoughts after Him." Moreover,
the preacher's task is to help our age see through the fallacy that
the chief aim of civilization is the destruction of pain, the removal
of suffering, and the enthronement of ease and comfort as the

highest good of life. Release from pain is shouted at us from the radio and television, stares at us from subway cards and platform placards, fills our favorite magazines and newspapers. Not a few disciples of the cult have even invaded the pulpit and unhappily found it profitable for themselves.

Suffering has meaning, and pain is an integral part of all existence. Life begins in the pain of childbirth. It grows and develops through the disciplining of the body and the mind. It surmounts obstacles by rising above tragedy, suffering, and sorrow. It deepens the spirit and broadens the vision by making the pain of others its own. The birth of every new idea is like childbirth—painful. But nothing is more powerful than a new idea, though born in pain, when its time has come. Sometimes it is only through suffering that men learn the great lessons of life. Without the pain of God and the suffering of Jesus, there can be no redemption of the world.

However, it is the preacher's task to help men know why their civilization, which prided itself on its achievements in the realms of science, art and culture, often becomes a hell on earth. Without ethical considerations and the humility to mold ourselves and our time to the will of God, moral chaos is an inevitable result. Fortunately, an increasing number of people seem to be taking the preacher more seriously. The writer of Ecclesiastes was at the center of the true and faithful minister's task when he wrote, "Because the preacher was wise, he still taught the people knowledge; yea, he gave good heed, and sought out, and set in order many proverbs." (ECCLESIASTES 12:9)

In recent years church membership and attendance has greatly increased and is still increasing by leaps and bounds. But there is no evidence yet of a corresponding moral and religious influence on personal, corporate, national, or international life. Undoubtedly there is some, though by no means enough. Whatever the motives for church increase, the picture is one of hope. However this great influx into the church developed, it demonstrates that people are disturbed, that they lack faith in themselves and seek a better and a surer way of life. Recognizing the need for the all-embodying power of God to achieve a better life and a decent world must precede the establishment of a happier world and a finer life. Contrition must always precede salvation. A quotation from Charles A. Lindbergh's book, *Of Flight and Life,* is more than significant at this point:

> To me, in my youth, science was more important than either man or God. I worshipped science . . . I was awed by its knowledge. Its advances had surpassed man's wildest dreams. In its learning seemed to lie the key to all the mysteries of life.
>
> It took many years for me to discover that science, with all its brilliancy, lights only a middle chapter of creation. I saw the science I worshipped, and the aircraft I loved, destroying the civilization I expected them to serve, and which I thought was as permanent as earth itself.
>
> Now I realize that to survive, one must look beyond the speed and power of aircraft, and beyond the material strength of science. And though God cannot be seen as tangibly as I had demanded as a child, His presence can be seen in every sight and act and incident. Now I know that when man loses this sense, he misses the true quality of life. . . . He loses the infinite strength without which no people can survive—the element which war cannot defeat or peace corrupt.
>
> Now I understand that spiritual truth is more essential to a nation than the mortar in its cities' walls. For when the actions of all people are unguided by these truths, it is only a matter of time before the walls themselves collapse.
>
> The most urgent mission of our time is to understand these truths, and to apply them to our way of modern life.[3]

To which we can all say amen. But then we must quickly ask, "Who but the preacher is to lead man to this knowledge, this awareness of the limitations of science, and the dangers of its use in the hands of evil and sinful men?" What a time for urgent and adventurous preaching of the gospel, when God is revealing Himself in such an infinite variety of ways, and by these revelations is giving man a larger share in the universe! It is the glory of the preacher's task to help rouse men to the consciousness of the largest human responsibilities they have ever had under the moral and divine judgment of God. Neither the advance of science nor the arrogance of secularism can cancel out the urgent need of the high commission to which the preacher has been called.

The preacher is still in the business of redemption, with a greater responsibility than ever before. His place may be different, but his opportunity is greatly enhanced. If he will break through his isolation and speak boldly to the needs of this hour, we may yet see the salvation of the Lord. Despite the calloused sophistication of our age, there is a great hunger for the Way. It is the hunger which the eunuch had in the eighth chapter of Acts when he replied to Philip, "How can I [understand] except some man should guide me?" If we would preach without fear and favor and with the intelligence and power as Philip did, the results would be the same.

It is vastly more difficult to preach to a nation flush with a succession of victories and surfeited with material success than to a nation humiliated by disaster and defeat; but it has to be done. God demands that His ministers do it, otherwise we may come to deify ourselves, to believe ourselves invincible—the chosen people who can do no wrong—the elect of God who make God a captive of our imagination.

Millions want a faith to live by, but "how can they hear without a preacher?" as St. Paul asked in the tenth chapter of Romans, "and how shall they preach except they be sent?" As it is written, "How beautiful are the feet of them that preach the gospel of peace and bring glad tidings of good things." The good news is that God still undergirds the world, that when we are amenable to His will He uses us to holy purposes, and when we thwart His will by arrogance, sin and conceit He breaks us; and that no possible combination of the powers of evil or the forces of history can thwart His will. Let this be our message of assurance and warning.

It is an awful truth that at the height of our vaunted achievements of art, education and science we have seen more bestial inhumanity, destructive wars, rampant political corruption, widespread violence and anxiety, and suffering of the human mind than any other time in history. There would be some comfort for us, no doubt, if this situation had been limited to the so-called backward people. But the saddest truth of all is the fact that this degradation occurred among the most enlightened, and in the very heart of Christian lands.

It is also an awful truth that lack of moral and religious direction leaves men grossly deficient in spiritual ways no matter how brilliant and proficient they are in material terms. Men must still reestablish the harmonious relationship among themselves which God prefigured in the orderly relationships among the planets, the atoms, and the molecules. It is true that man has tried to rearrange these planets, atoms, and molecules, but life organized apart from God's righteous demands and motivated by a power and culture independent of moral considerations is bound to end in chaos. Elton Trueblood, in his book *The Predicament of Modern Man*, put the problem very succinctly when he wrote:

> The lesson of our time is that this delusion is no better than any other delusion. The problem will not take care of itself. Unless the spiritual problem is solved, civilization will fail; indeed, we already have a foretaste of that failure in many parts of the world. Man's sinful nature is such that he will use instruments of power for evil ends unless there is something to instruct him in their beneficent uses. Without the conscious and intelligent buttressing of what has been demonstrated as precious, human society goes down. . . . Beasts do not need a philosophy or a religion, but man does.[4]

Everyone has to develop a philosophy of life and religion which satisfactorily answers two questions: "What must I do with my life —with the power, the knowledge, the wealth, and the leisure which modern advance puts at my disposal? And when life tumbles in, how do I keep my equilibrium and reinstate my life without going to pieces?"

These are religious and moral questions which our society poses more urgently for us today than ever before. Unless men can find adequate and satisfying answers to them, they destroy both themselves and their society. Whether modern men know it or not, they need the message of religious hope and discipline more than ever before. There may well be some who would like to place the whole blame for the isolation of the preacher at the door of the secularists. This is all too easy an escape, for the religious forces have great tendencies toward isolation within themselves. The process of isolation begins almost from the moment a young man recognizes the call to the ministry. The holiness of being set apart by the laying on of hands can be devastatingly misleading unless rightly understood. Next the candidate is surrounded by the local church, the ecclesiastical bodies. He often lives and moves in the too limited and narrow circle of his fellow associates. His apparel may accentuate his separation. He retreats to his study where he can be surrounded by his books, for he has learned to love the cloistered quietness of the seminary. He remembers how professors urged him to make adequate preparation for the sermon, and he has come to believe that preaching alone and above all else is the preacher's supreme task.

He may even come to glorify his loneliness and to feel he of all men is in the tradition of the heroes and saints of old, forgetting entirely that no man ever became a saint in bed or in his study, but only in the life stream—where the saint was the messenger of God to men and women in trouble and to a world in travail.

The preacher, above all other people, runs the risk of overestimating personal isolation or of making personal judgment on the foibles and fickleness of human nature. He runs the danger of such an unconscious arrogance in separateness that he may not have time for the children and youth of the church—"they don't understand anyway," or for Sunday School teachers—"it takes too much time to instruct them, and besides, they are a rather secondary appendage to the preaching." He may even consider *wor-ship* secondary to preaching.

It is difficult to escape the pride of being admired by the congregation, and even more difficult to transfer their love for us up to God. We are not enough in ourselves. People need something higher. It is not easy to escape from the pride of elation when people praise our meager efforts. It is very easy to believe that we are as good as the people often tell us we are. To keep Jesus ever in front, "Not I but the Father who sent me." There is always the temptation to feel crushed on a rainy Sunday because many parishioners will be absent from church. We cannot overcome these temptations by ourselves. Only God can save us from ourselves.

The seminary gives the candidate for the ministry special direction; he becomes proficient in a terminology of religion, which to the ordinary layman is a language with passwords which serve to admit clergymen to the inner circle of the elect, but cannot be understood by laymen. Hence, a problem of communication of preacher to people begins very early. Young preachers, anxious to vindicate the seminary's efforts in training them to establish their place with the congregation, eager to appear erudite to great theological minds of the time, are seriously afflicted with this problem. It isolates them from the very people whom God calls them to serve.

Theology, just as every other field of special study, has its own terminology. The terminology by which theology's deepest truth and most expansive ideas are expressed is foreign to the average person of good education, just as in the case of medicine or chemistry or physics. However, the doctor seldom addresses groups other than his colleagues, who have the same background of training and experience, whereas the preacher must spend most of his time preaching to groups of people assembled from the most diverse backgrounds possible. Every profession, age, and education level, social and political group are represented in the average church. These people are unfamiliar with the language of theology. Our language of religion can, and often does, become a barrier which laymen have a hard time breaking through.

Every minister needs to give serious and careful thought to the problem of communication. Most laymen are too embarrassed or too respectful to tell us when they are baffled by our terminology. It is not easy to express great theological ideas of life and faith in simple language, but it is possible if we work hard enough at it. Most people could say to us what a storekeeper said to his pastor at the conclusion of an address at a Rotary Club luncheon, "I wish I could understand you on Sundays as easily as I understood you today. Why can't ministers be that simple and direct in the pulpit?"

I told a story in my autobiography, *Road Without Turning,* which will bear repeating on these pages.[5] During the first three months of my ministry I felt frustrated by the older people who seemed silently to ask me, as I rose to deliver the sermon each Sunday, "Well, young man, what are you going to tell us this morning?" As faculty members from Columbia University and Union Seminary were usually in the congregation, I decided to preach on a series of six profound theological subjects. This, I decided, would show the congregation how fortunate they were in having me as their pastor, and would let the learned professors know how much I had absorbed. I got through the first three sermons largely because few of the congregation knew what I was talking about, and also because the teachers were no longer grading my efforts. For the fourth sermon, I chose the topic "The Ontological Argument for the Proof of the Existence of God." Then for fear that this title would not sufficiently confound the long-suffering fold, I added a sub-topic, "Discussed from the point of view of Anselm, Descartes and Kant."

At the close of the service, one of our faithful deacons invited me to her home for supper. After the meal she said, gently, "You know, Pastor Robinson, you are a young preacher and we all love you, but for goodness sake, if you take us step by step and begin where we are, we'll follow you. They taught you theology, psychology, and philosophy in the seminary, but you haven't learned any 'peopleology.' You've been trying to give us in three weeks what you learned in three years. Next Sunday morning, preach about something that we know something about, and give us just a little something new." Then with a little smile and her face half turned away she added, "It would be well if you preached on something you know about, too."

No! God never leaves Himself without a witness, and that deacon was His witness. Preachers need to listen, for God speaks through many voices. A great deal of nonsense is talked about the inarticulateness of uneducated and uninformed laymen. Never isolate yourself from them. Never look down in condescension upon them, for you can learn much from them. They, too, are in the great Protestant tradition of the priesthood of all believers.

It was Rosetti in his sonnet entitled *Moderation and Tolerance* who said:

> Let no man to o'erweening pride be wrought,
> But count his state as fortune's gift and due.
> He is a fool who deems that none has sought,
> The truth, save he alone, or knows it true.
>
> .   .   .   .   .
>
> To each was portioned the breath of God,
> Who gave them divers instincts from one source.

As we preach and minister under the judgment of God in these troublesome days, what then shall we do with our preaching? Shall we make it an ecclesiastical showplace to obtain position, adulation, and popularity, and live on the weekly trek from study to pulpit and back again? Shall we make each pastorate an ecclesiastical waystop while we angle for a larger and more influential pulpit, or labor joyously in unostentatious places at the pleasure of God and for the redemption of the souls which are precious in His sight? Shall we stay on the balcony of religion with a small select company, or join Jesus in the roadway with the men and women he came to seek and to save? Shall we let the forces of the secular world fence us in by too easy an accommodation to its mores, or shall we thrust ourselves upon the mercy of God who

called us, and let Him use us to help break the moral impasse
brought on by the power-complex of scientific secularism? Shall
we always preach with the intellectual genius of a mental gym-
nast so that we may receive the praise of our fellow ministers,
or shall we feed the hungering flock of God with the simple
bread of life so that even a child can understand?

Shall we limit our service to a specialized role by professionaliz-
ing our ministry and compel the flock to come to us, or shall we
follow the injunction of the bishop in the Episcopal church when
he ordained a young man to the deaconate, "You are to go seek
out the poor, bereaved, troubled, and hungered"?

One of the most essential differences between Christianity
and the other living religions of the world is this: "In all the others,
the central theme is man seeking God, while in ours it is God
seeking man." We expect more of ourselves because God demands more of us, and we are accountable to His exacting tri-
bunal of judgment. If our preaching is to be a revealing ministry,
it must grow out of involvement with people in their search for
God's will in their lives. Otherwise, it becomes highly irrelevant.

Preaching may be defined as truth through personality, but a
personality which touches life at every point. I once heard Bishop
Stephen Neill of London say at the University of Toronto, when
I was an associate missioner with him there a few years back,
"Touch Christ anywhere, and you always touch life." The woman
in the crowd managed to touch only the hem of Jesus' garment
as he passed by, and she was healed. *But Jesus was in the crowd,
and that is why she could touch him.* If we are truly in Christ then
people touch him through us. Great preaching, except for a few
choice souls who are richly endowed with brilliant minds and
warm hearts, is a result of a great pastorate of the people.

In my days as a student at seminary I was often dismayed that so
many of my classmates wanted to be little facsimiles of Buttrick,
Scherer, Sockman, Fosdick, and Coffin all rolled into one. Great
men, all these, and who of us would not like to be compared to
them? They are worthy of emulation. Few of us, however, can
attain the eminence they reached. Most of us will serve our

ministry to the end of our days in humble parishes and receive salaries which barely keep us above the border line of debt. But we can know that most of the saintly giants of the pulpit, after whom we wish to pattern our lives, would have served in places like ours without complaint and with fidelity, had God ordained it so. They climbed to their positions by being, first of all, great pastors of the flock.

But hardly anyone in my class at seminary wanted to be a great pastor. In fact, the term was seldom used.

The living proof of what constitutes a truly great preacher was there in our midst in the towering person of Henry Sloane Coffin, the president of the seminary at the time.

Good preaching does not just happen, and it cannot be induced by cleverness. It is a result of an agonizing pursuit of man and of God. Such had characterized Dr. Coffin's ministry. It was Dr. Walter Russell Bowie who said, "The real preacher is more than a maker of sermons." I can set before you no better example of the preacher in these times who labors under the judgment of God, than Dr. Coffin. When he died, those of us who knew him felt that something supremely good had gone from the earth.

When a student at Yale, he used his summers to work among the Indians on the Shinnecock Reservation. At Edinburgh he played a portable organ in the streets of the slums, and rallied the crowd by hymn-singing before preaching to them out there in the open air. Back at Union he gave himself, beyond his studies, to neighborhood work. In his two pastorates before his call to presidency of Union, he was the devoted and faithful pastor of his flock, rich and poor alike, he was the unreserved companion and counselor of his staff, and the champion of his Sunday School teachers.

He preached exciting and meaningful sermons to children every Sunday. His preaching stirred the hearts, lifted the vision, and won men, women, and college students to the banners of Christ everywhere. He knew the strength and weakness of our time, and he was an equal match for the secularists who tried to wring the world dry of the tears of God without so much as recognizing that sinful man could manipulate the secularists' vaunted theories to his own nefarious end.

"Uncle Henry," as he was known affectionately to two generations of students, knew not only the modern theories and movements of scientific, social, economic, and political change; he was intimately acquainted with the secular as well as the religious leaders of his day. He kept abreast of his time without sacrificing his responsibilities as a pastor.

Dr. Bowie wrote of Dr. Coffin in a little book entitled *This Ministry*, "Men seek for God because, as has been nobly stated, they want 'light on the mystery of life, and strength for the mastery of life.' "[6] Dr. Coffin was such a preacher of the mysteries of God that he placed the light and the strength of God in the hearts of thousands. Yet with it all, this dynamic servant of God and compassionate friend of men was approachable by all. His humility was infectious.

The preacher under judgment is faithful to the call to relate men, in whatever circumstances they may find themselves, to "an other" Who is God. The preacher is the symbol of God's untiring love for His children. "I taught Ephraim how to walk; I carried him as a babe in my arms. I cannot let him go." This is God's judgment of love as the redeeming power unto salvation. The preacher may preach the justice of God, the righteous wrath of God, the omnipotence of God, but he must also preach the love of God, "for God so loved the world that He gave His only begotten son." Always, and in all situations, the preacher must exemplify that love in his life and his action as well as in his preaching.

Elizabeth Yates, in her prize-winning children's book, *Amos Fortune*, has told the story of a former slave by that name, who purchased his freedom and settled in Jaffrey, New Hampshire, and became the respected tanner of the town. Amos Fortune's daughter was permitted to go to school, but she was often the butt of cruel mockery. When he went to church he had to sit in a segregated gallery and was never admitted to the administration of Holy Communion. Amos Fortune bore his hurt nobly. When he died he left a part of his savings to the town school, and a share to the Congregational church for the purchase of a silver communion service, beautiful and good enough for that holy moment where all should be as one. What a judgment of love was this last will and testament of an unlettered former slave. It stands as a goal toward which all ministers of the gospel may aspire. The citizens of Jaffrey, a century and a half late, paid tribute to Amos Fortune by establishing a distinguished series of forum lectures to the memory of his love—a love which outlasted the prejudice of his peers.

We are under judgment to be the living proof of the all-embracing power of God's eternal love.

II

THE FELLOWSHIP
OF CONFESSION

I

CHRISTIAN fellowship is a confident family relationship created by God, sustained by the love of Christ, and made continuous by the Holy Spirit.

Through it, we share both our triumphs over evil and our defeats by sin, and through it we find the spiritual resources which enable us to penetrate life's perplexities.

Christianity is no set of rules to be observed in isolation; it is a vital relationship to history, man, and God. And within it, there is an adventure to be found—an adventure with God and our fellowmen. This is the fellowship of confession.

For the minister, the fellowship of confession means a trinity of relationships. The first is all-important—his confessional fellowship with God. The second is familiar—the confessional fellowship of those who come to the minister for guidance, comfort, and support. The third is rare—it is the confessional fellowship of those to whom the minister himself must turn in his own times of trouble.

Just as our own prior encounter with God through Christ determines the effectiveness of our witness to those who look to us for help, so does it create and sustain the humility necessary to confess our own sins in the hearing of a brother confessor. Yet while all ministers have some experience with the first two confessional relationships, few of us have had more than an occasional, fleeting experience with the third. But without it, the equation is incomplete, the essential trinity of relationships is unfulfilled.

In our awareness of God, we preachers find the source of strength and power. A man who is not God-centered can function in the ministry for decade after decade without ever becoming an effective witness for God. The preacher is a conveyor of truth. Truth like water can flow through any kind of pipe, just as electricity passes through any kind of wire. But the effectiveness of the supply depends upon the condition of the conductor. The pipe can get clogged, and wires have resistance. God does not reveal sublime truth to small minds, for He does not deal in trivialities.

In the second of his three relationships, the minister finds his largest and most important area of work—shepherding the flock, especially those who have fallen into error or made a mess of their lives. And since the minister is a normal, mortal man, he is subject to the same fallacies which afflict all other human beings who have fallen short of the glory of God.

I have deliberately coupled the word "confession" with "fellowship." This makes it a mutually-dependent relationship. All of us are dependent upon God, and not He upon us. Obviously, I do not use the word confession in the usual sense of our Roman Catholic brethren, where the priest has power to pronounce absolution. He acts as the agent in the removal of guilt. As I use the term, there is nothing obligatory about confession, nor does it presuppose that there must be regular stated intervals for spiritual inventory, nor that the church should require penalties if it is ignored. The "penalties" which come to us are a natural consequence of our refusal to use a means of grace which is so close at hand. The result is often a shriveled soul and a wrecked personality.

No, I use the word "confession" in the larger sense of a voluntary, open, and sincere acknowledgment of guilt to God, to the minister, or to a confidential Christian brother, and it includes the idea of a drawing together in love for strength and spiritual growth. To confession I have added the word "fellowship," because the latter is a distinctly Christian idea not found in any of the other living religions of the world. Christian fellowship is created by the desire of God to draw all men into the family of His spirit, and to show them their mutual dependence. It is a fellowship kept alive by the Holy Spirit and made responsive by faith. Charles Kean, in his book, *Making Sense Out of Life*, has rightly stated:

> Within this fellowship men need not fear the pressure
> of their past mistakes, nor need they fear the unknowable
> and unforeseeable decisions which lie ahead.[1]

The high calling of the minister, as a revealer of the truth of God and an interpreter of the meaning and reason of existence, demands a constant surrender of our lives that we may be clear and faithful channels of God's love, mercy, and grace. As Bishop Gerald Kennedy told the students at Southwestern University:

> We no longer preach ourselves or our accomplishments.
> We are not pleaders for an organization or promoters
> of special programs. We are witnesses for Christ, knowing at last that in him there is the light men need to live
> by.

If that mind is to be in us—that mind which, as St. Paul said, was "in Christ Jesus"—then we must draw ever closer to Christ so that we may be closer to God. There is no substitute for the deepening of the devotional life of a minister; and there is no magic religious ritual which can lead us to clarity of thought, purity of heart, gentleness of spirit, direction of mind, largeness of soul, and sureness of purpose. The only sure way is the practice of the presence of God in some quiet retreat, where we stand in a confessional relationship to God as "empty pitchers before a full fountain." The preacher who lives and walks close to God is usually a minister of tremendous spiritual resources and power.

God is always desirous of breaking through to reveal His truth to our wayward world, and He uses human instruments to convey this truth. But the instrument must be pure and humble to be of use to God. Purity of heart is more important than intellectual capacity; willingness to wait and listen is a more valuable asset than facility of speech; and depth and humility of spirit is worth more than renown or pulpits of great fame. Isaiah recognized the necessity of cleansing himself.

To be sure, God often uses as witnesses men who are not paragons of virtue. The point is, however, that when they are good enough and holy enough, God's purpose can be clearly revealed in and through their lives. Hence, the angel took the live coals of God's righteousness to cleanse the lips of Isaiah when he cried out in distress, "I am a man of unclean lips, and I dwell in the midst of a people of unclean lips." After this purification, Isaiah rose up as prophet without equal in all human history. In no other part of the Bible is there so clear a view of the promise of redemption and the grace of God. Isaiah lived so close to the love and the mind of God that God used him to reveal His messages for sixty years and more.

Consecration is a surrender of soul, mind, and heart to the will of God. It is a discipline of the spirit and the body to the purposes of God in our lives. Those of us who speak for God must be consecrated to God. Otherwise, we cannot see and hear rightly enough to catch heavenly illuminations, nor speak clearly and with enough authority for men to understand us. Otherwise, what we say is likely to be more an interpretation of our own ideas than the judgment of God. It is all too easy to slip unconsciously from "thus saith the Lord" to "thus say I"! Many a preacher is often guilty of committing this grievous error without being aware of it. The danger is always present. Nothing but discipline of pride and self to the will and majesty of God can save us.

It is easy indeed to become blinded by the wisdom of our own conceit, and so deeply involved in our own thoughts that we simply cannot see through the false veneer of self-righteousness, and so be able to present our "bodies a living sacrifice, holy, acceptable unto God." (ROMANS 12:1)

The right to say, "Thus saith the Lord" is not conferred with the degree from a seminary, nor effected by a process of osmosis during the laying on of hands in the ceremony of ordination. It is merited by a pure life, consecration of self, discipline of mind and soul, faithful listening, and a willingness to be amenable to the will of God.

There is an even greater danger, however, when the thoughts of others are made to sound like the voice of the Lord. In this day of modern mass communication, which Dr. Halford Luccock calls "a babble of tongues" in his book, *Communicating the Gospel*,[2] we little realize how greatly our thinking and preaching is twisted, contorted and conditioned by experts with a bias who shout at us morning, noon, and night.

Our parishioners are spared no more than the rest of us. They too are prey to the opinions, the snobbisms, the mercenary standards, the selfish goals which are part and parcel of their favorite entertainment. What *we* must give them is no electronic voice, but our clearest inspirations, uncluttered by slogans and clichés, and uncontrolled by sponsors; and our devotion, speaking out of hearts and minds which know the heart and mind of God because we live close to the heart of God. God does not need parrots, He needs prophets and priests.

The preacher needs to get away from words, electrically magnified, and spend many hours off with himself, with his Bible, a hymnbook and the vigil of prayer, listening to the voice of God as it speaks to his conscience in the light of vision. Peter's affirmation of Jesus as the Christ had nothing vicarious about it, as Jesus himself knew. "Blessed art thou Simon Barjona: for flesh and blood hath not revealed it unto thee, but my Father which is in heaven." (ST. MATTHEW 16:17)

The minister's task is a difficult one. If he takes his call seriously he is always presented with more than he can possibly do. First come the demands of persons whose claims are urgent and immediate, then follows the necessity for keeping the machinery of the church in motion, and afterwards the demands of the denomination. The problems of what to do *when*, the relative emphasis, the need to know what should and should not be neglected—these do not have easy and ready solutions. Every day is a day not of one but of many decisions. But the most important decision regards the purpose of our lives as preachers of the Word, and God's requirement of us.

So much is demanded of the preacher in these hectic and difficult days of trouble and chance that devotional requirements are usually, all too frequently, pushed aside. Reading to prepare a sermon or a talk, or reading for sheer personal enjoyment is sometimes thought of as a substitute for personal devotion and meditation. Sometimes we are tempted to believe that the weekly preachers' meeting or our meetings with brother clergymen at denominational headquarters are sufficient devotional exercise. True, many of our activities are both good and unavoidable. But after taking due cognizance of our obligations in the work of our ministry, we are under the eternal compunction to set primary importance on our own spiritual growth and private worship. Here is the great source supply of our strength.

The minister is particularly vulnerable to the temptation to let his personal growth suffer. He is under constant pressure to produce, create, and pour himself out, with little time left for refilling.

He leads the worship of the church, but is often so involved in the mechanics that he himself may not worship successfully. He makes prayer and the inner life an object of study, and tries to help his congregation see how and why it is imperative, but his own prayers and devotional practice may be shallow. He persuades his leaders and teachers to study the lives of the saints and reformers, but he seldom seeks to emulate them.

Protestant clergymen are so greatly motivated by activity that a retreat to the inner sanctum of the soul, in some place set apart for the purpose, is all but forgotten. The modern world views this sort of emphasis upon the consecrated devotional life as something quaint. In fact, the average preacher considers such retiring from the busy round of daily duties and the weekly activities of the church as either impossible to accomplish or an indulgence. Others view the time they steal from the crush of programs, meetings, services, discussion groups, and church business with a sense of guilt.

Time taken for personal devotion and private retreat, for the peace of the soul and the mind, should never give the minister a feeling of guilt. When he is out of touch with himself and with God, he cannot be in very effectual touch with his fellow men. I have always been impressed by one of the younger clergymen on our staff at the Church of the Master, whom I have often found in meditation and prayer when I have unlocked the church before the custodian arrived. He was perhaps seeking the peace of soul and singleness of purpose about which Anne Morrow Lindbergh has written so beautifully in her gracious little book, *Gift from the Sea*:

> But I want first of all—in fact, as an end to these other desires—to be at peace with myself. I want a single-ness of eye, a purity of intention, a central core to my life that will enable me to carry out those obligations and activities as well as I can. I want, in fact—to borrow from the language of the saints—to live 'in grace' as much of the time as possible. I am not using this term in a strictly theological sense. By grace I mean an inner harmony, essentially spiritual, which can be translated into out-ward harmony. I am seeking perhaps what Socrates asked for in the prayer from the *Phaedrus* when he said, 'May the outward and inward man be at one.' I would like to achieve a state of inner spiritual grace from which I could function and give as I was meant to in the eye of God.[3]

The demands of the community upon the preacher take up where the demands of the church leave off. Unless the minister is wise and disciplined, he will fall into the error of becoming more of a community leader than a minister. Such temptations are often enormous, for the very respect he wins by his life and his position makes him a man sought out to head committees, boards and drives. Furthermore, if he is keenly interested in and aware of all the problems of his community, it is certain that other churches, unions, organizations, and groups will demand him as a speaker. In this situation the minister sometimes suspects that he has been called upon primarily to represent God's "endorsement" of man's little campaigns. When he refuses, when he protests that he needs time for his own work and his own devotional life, he is told—even by sincere people—that this extra bit of public relations will "help his ministry and his church." My own considerable experience indicates that it does "help" up to a point—but how soon that point is reached!

Many a preacher has allowed popularity and success to stunt the spiritual growth of his soul, and interfere with the shepherding of the flock. Popularity is a misleading mistress. Her applause may be too-easily won; even if earned, her praise and attentions are fickle. And above all, there is the danger of becoming a religious idol. When the crowd tires of one idol, it seeks another to worship. Too often it does not note in its first flush of enthusiasm that the leader has been created by clever publicity. Too often the crowd assembles about a leader just as crowds form in a city street—a cluster of four or five attracts still more to gape and gather, and yet even more until the street is blocked. The crowd-mentality runs first after one idol and then another—just as in Jesus' time, when it ran first after John and then after Jesus. Even John was affected by the crowd, for in despair he sent a message to Jesus, "Are you he that should come, or do we look for another?" To which Jesus, ever conscious of the fickleness of the multitude, inquired, after he had made adequate reply to John, "What went ye out . . . to see? A reed shaken with the wind?" (ST. MATTHEW 11:7)

If the preacher protects his time by refusing most outside engagements, he may be looked upon as a narrow-minded separationist, selfishly concerned only with the salvation of those in his flock. Obviously we must demonstrate our interest and concern in the welfare of the community—but we are not called to be neighborhood errand boys! Jesus put the record straight for all time when he said, "But what went ye out for to see? A prophet? Yea, I say unto you, and more than a prophet. For this is he, of whom it is written, Behold I send my messenger before thy face, which shall prepare thy way before thee." (ST. MATTHEW 11:9–10)

As messengers of God we have a central purpose to keep, despite the multitude of distractions, no matter how worthy they may be. Our purpose is ever a venture with God, Whom we seek to make real and vital, as we venture with people in the ways of God. Only by searching our own hearts and seeking constantly for an extra portion of the grace and wisdom of God can we come anywhere near being a living and adequate witness for God, Who commissioned us to the task.

Beyond the necessary obligations of our calling, and the pull of society to countless other tasks, are the burdens of personal trouble which may keep us from rightful concern with the quieter devotions. Then still further there are those who come to us for guidance, or the hopelessly sick, waiting patiently in pain. Or there are those whose faith we help to sustain. Or the recalcitrant church official, whose irritation we must bear and whose love we seek to win. Or the heartbroken, who wish us to find the means to save a home from breaking up. Above all, there is the burden of our own sense of failure after preaching a sermon, and the knowledge of having fallen from grace in a time of weakness, even though perhaps no one else knows it but God. Few communicants of a church ever fully appreciate the tremendous burdens imposed by the confidences a pastor carries in his heart and on his mind.

These trials so intrude upon our minds that they often serve to keep us from private devotion. But on the contrary, they should serve to throw us back upon God for help. We cannot bear them alone—nor do we have to—because He bears them with us. It is easy to distrust our own abilities; and apparently it is just as easy to forget that we have resources at hand for the asking. If we presume to speak for God when people are in trouble (and this is more than a mere presumption) then we must practice the conscientious outreach of the soul for God, we must exact a response, and we must be willing to throw ourselves unreservedly upon God for support.

When any clergyman honestly looks inward upon his soul to the recesses of his own heart, he sees disclosed in it his fears, anxieties, secret and unholy thoughts, perplexities, inadequacies, ambitions, and desires. He sees how great is his need for the help of God for himself and for those who make no pretense of living as close to dependence upon God as he does. In this respect, preachers need to use great discernment, lest they fall into the error of Pharisees and Sadducees who believed that by consistent moral effort alone they could reach the ideal. The minister at least should know that without the help of God, he is powerless to reach the goal of religious living which God demands of all of us. A line from an old hymn my mother used to sing made an indelible impression upon me: "The moral man came to the judgment, but his self-righteous rags would not do."

Jesus did not trust his wisdom to the limit of his own capacity; he constantly sought divine guidance. He pushed off from the shore in a boat, climbed the steep hills, went up upon the housetop early in the morning, kept vigil with God in the wilderness, climbed to the summit of the Mount of Transfiguration to be alone with God, examine his own motives, gain strength, withstand temptation; he sought the solitude of the desert to talk with and to listen to God. Each of these retreats from the hustle of life —even from the work of kingdom-building—was for our Lord an experience of confirmation and healing. The preacher who labors in the Lord's vineyard today stands no less in need of the healing presence of God, Who is always closer than hands and feet. We do not need to cry out with Job in anguish, "Oh, that I knew where I might find Him," for He is omnipresent, He is waiting to be invited into the intimacy of our lives whenever we make conditions right to receive Him.

It is certain that all great literature, great poetry, great music are, in one form or another, revelations of God. It is equally certain that no poet or musician who did not yield himself and his creative impulse to the voice of the Eternal has ever left a valuable contribution. It is, therefore, all the more certain that the man who speaks for God must yield himself up wholly to the service of God.

God indeed speaks through the poet and the musician, but in limited areas. Through the minister he speaks the truth of God to the whole of life. It was Ruskin who argued that the minister has an ultimate obligation to the knowledge and the maintenance of the truth so that a mirror may be held up by which our lives are examined and improved. Dwight L. Moody, whose prodigious good works spanned half a century and encircled the earth, was sustained by an ordered devotional life of periodic retreat into the presence of God. He once said, "The world has yet to see what God can do with that man who fully surrenders his life to Him." This could refer to any one of us. We need to turn to God daily for assurance before speaking, but only a disciplined Christian can do this.

"The world is too much with us," as Wordsworth wrote a long time back before our day of haste. We live at such a fast "clip," amid so much chatter and noise, that God has very little chance to be with us. And when He does speak, we often cannot hear Him above the clamor. If we need time to think, surely we need time to worship and pray. It is possible for a minister to become insensitive and unreceptive to the voice of God. Woe unto us if the judgment of God should ever find us unreceptive and unavailable. Bishop Gerald Kennedy, in the chapter on the Saints in his book, *With Singleness of Heart,* has written a word of competent spiritual advice to ministers:

> Action is all very well, but it must be directed toward
> the right goals and have a spiritual quality within it. Men
> who give their lives to doing, without consideration of
> their aims, are not the possessors of the future. It is

amazing how quickly they are forgotten, and how un-
forgettable are the neglected ones who established some
advance in the realm of the spirit.[4]

The reason that quiet men of spiritual depth enriched their time
and ours can be seen in a comment on "the significance of silence," by Leslie Weatherhead, in his book by that title:

> One is glad to find that even the busy Paul has a word
> to those eager Thessalonians: "Study to be quiet"; and
> we need that quiet not that we may think more posi-
> tively, whipping our minds to activity, or to do more and
> more, spurring our wills to greater effort, but that we
> may, in quiescent relaxation of mind, receive and com-
> mune.[5]

What I suggest is not a slavish allegiance to a fetish of inflexible
exercises or to a static sitting with tools and implements of worship, but rather an attitude of mind, a condition of the heart, a
desire of the soul for the real presence of God, and a discipline
of the will and body to the central purpose of our calling. Devotional books help; the Bible is necessary but not always indispensable; and a place set apart is valuable but not mandatory. The Holy
of Holies is in a pure heart which strives daily to be a more fit
habitation for the presence of God. We can retire to it in the
spirit no matter where we are—whether on a plane, a boat, a street
car, or walking in the woods. For the minister it can be his study,
the pew of an empty church, a path in the hills, or a bench in the
park. The practice of the presence of God is similar to what Emerson said in one of his essays:

> You may search the whole world over for the good,
> the beautiful, the true, but unless you take it with you,
> you cannot find it.

The preacher's greatest need is a vital and living fellowship
with God. True peace of heart, mind, and soul is not attained by
the manipulation of any tools of devotion or therapy, but by a profound and all-inclusive religious experience of great dimensions

which transforms us enough so that we may see God within us.

I have no authority save that of the Lord God. It is neither my education, my experience, nor my denomination which gives power to my life and efficacy to my words. It is only the mind and knowledge of God, which I see through a glass imperfectly, but strive daily to see more clearly. Because I know this need for myself, I dare suggest it as a great need for all ministers and also for our laymen.

I first felt this need soon after I was convinced of my call to the ministry, when I passed an Episcopal church in Cleveland, Ohio, and saw a sign on the door—ENTER, REST AND PRAY. I did, and came out refreshed and inspired. The need for a closer walk with God, the need for boldness to confess ashamedly but confidently my shortcomings, to place myself frankly before Him for chastening and cleasing, to ask for forgiveness and renewal, to seek deeper insight and heightened inspiration, and to find guidance, strength, and the grace of humility, does not grow less with time and experience. With experience and time, many areas are improved; temptations are more easily mastered. But more of God's power in our lives is always necessary. The most saintly man is one who constantly craves more of God's mercy, wisdom, and grace.

Protestant clergymen have not done enough to develop the private devotional life either for themselves or for their parishioners. May the time not be long in coming when greater stress will be put on the development of the inner life; for this is the way God changes the world—by changing people. The religion of Jesus is not an outward garment but an inward growth of spirit, which nevertheless changes the outer man. And changed men help change society!

The need to develop retreat centers for the teaching and practice of inner communion is at least as urgent as the building of places for conferences, discussion, and study groups. Perhaps they are even more important precisely because we have done so little to answer a need which is so great.

And the need is as great for our communicants as for ourselves

—yet we cannot lead them until we know the road. Personal devotion which leads to deepened insight and revealed knowledge is not limited to prophets and saints. There is nothing so mysterious or so deep about the development of the inner life that any consecrated layman cannot attain, in all its glorious illumination, if he earnestly seeks it.

In looking through pulpit manuals and books on the work of the ministry, one has to search far and wide to obtain material on the deepening of the inner life of the minister. Most of the works deal with subjects ranging from the choice of a wife, to what to do when the minister has the blues (an actual subdivision in one pastoral guide I read!), but very few of them offer any guidance for the great inner journey. It is not enough to assume that this is knowledge automatically presented to the minister with the call. I have had some of my most rewarding experiences with groups in my own congregation when we have gone on retreats, not to plan for the church year or to discuss vexing church problems, but to examine our spiritual welfare and to submit more fully to the spirit of God. I recall that a student on a retreat at Amherst College once said to the chaplain, John Coburn, after the period of silence for the day had been broken, "For the first time in my life I feel clean all over, inside and out."

Solitude in the presence of God is a blessed and wonderful state of being, a state which nourishes the soul and replenishes the springs of the spirit. When our own springs run dry we are helpless in the parched and barren wilderness. Anne Lindbergh is helpful to us again when she says:

> Yes, I felt closer to my fellow men too, even in my solitude. For it is not physical solitude that actually separates one from other men, not physical isolation, but spiritual isolation. It is not the desert island nor the stony wilderness that cuts you from the people you love. It is the wilderness in the mind, the desert wastes in the heart through which one wanders lost and a stranger. When one is a stranger to oneself then one is es-

tranged from others too. If one is out of touch with one-self, then one cannot touch others.[6]

II

Seward Hiltner begins the first chapter of his book, *Pastoral Counseling*, with the following paragraphs:

> In one congregation of a little less than a hundred people, there was a boy on parole from the state penitentiary who was trying "to go straight"—another on probation from the local police—a third who was flirting with a type of life that was bound to bring unhappiness and ruin—a young woman confused with intellectual doubts—a girl despondent over a broken love affair—a young couple who had just buried a child—a family where the mother had just died—a woman struggling with a morbid fear—a man who was desperately trying to overcome drink—a middle-aged couple whose home was going on the rocks—another couple who were worried over the conduct of their child—a young man who faced a serious operation within a month. If the minister had known his people better he would have undoubtedly been aware of other problems—these had consulted him.[7]

There are many who need us but cannot bring themselves to come to us, and there are many whose shallow existence we would like to help deepen into full life; but they successfully avoid us. Yet any pastor can find duplicates in his ministry for the situations described by Dr. Hiltner. Usually some three of every ten of the people whom the pastor shepherds are in need of insight, guidance, comfort, or support. Every pastor sometimes feels a sense of frustration and inadequacy when he tries to help people face their perplexing problems. The fellowship of confession—one could call it the fellowship of pastoral counseling—demands the largest single block of the minister's time. Yet theological seminaries have only recently begun to place a significant (though not yet large enough) emphasis upon this kind of training and guided experience during theological preparation.

In my seminary days the subject was hardly noticeable. There is some advance at the denominational level and considerably more among individual clergymen now, but still it is sadly superficial.

"Modern man is stranded," wrote Dr. Karl Stern, professor of psychiatry at the University of Ottawa, "but the preachers of the gospel are in danger of developing an 'I-told-you-so-if-you-only-had-followed-me' attitude. In practice this frequently leads to the situation that believers, the priest and levites of the parable, pass by while modern man, beaten and helpless in the ditch, has his wounds attended by some other fellow."[8]

Clinical training of the type initiated by the Council for Clinical Training, Inc., and the Institute of Pastoral Care need be greatly expanded and made an integral part of the theological training of all future ministers. These two groups, one with its headquarters in New York, and the other in Boston, have four goals—to enable the student to gain a fuller understanding of people—to help him discover effective methods of ministering to them—to help him work with other professions toward this end—and finally, to further our total insight into the problems of pastoral care in today's society.[9]

The tensions of the modern world are so great that we see all about us an almost pathological quest for security and peace of mind. Modern man is torn by economic and international insecurities, uncertain of the meaning and purpose of life in a world beset by ideological conflicts, and confused by the multitude of remedies ground out by politicians and statesmen. He is anxious about the increased technological power at his disposal; he is not at all sure that we know how to control it for the ultimate good of the world.

Fear and hysteria are never far away. Our mental hospitals are almost hopelessly overcrowded. There are thousands more outside of the institutions, men, women and children who suffer mental anguish but have never sought help, although their need is acute. These are the unfortunate people who are estranged from reality, or haunted by unreasonable fears—who do not love, who live in moral anxiety and are incapable of trusting those who love them. For them life is already hell on earth. Although their souls and bodies are not clothed in hospital garb, although their anguish is often carefully camouflaged—sensed rather than seen—their need for help is as great as many of those in institutions. The shallow, the frightened or frightening, timid or angry lives they lead might have been made free and productive if they could have obtained help early enough—if, for example, their pastors had been more alert and more capable.

Recognition of the growing need and importance of skillful counseling does not mean that the minister must look upon each of his parishioners as a potential mental or emotional case. That would be about as naive an assumption as the arguments of Lomar, Binet-Sangle, Rasmussen, and Hirsch in their attempt to classify Jesus as a psychopath—arguments which occasioned Dr. Albert Schweitzer's doctorate thesis, *The Psychiatric Study of Jesus*. There are many well adjusted, happy people in every congregation; otherwise, neither the church nor the nation could hang together with even minimum stability. However, at some rough spot along life's highway between birth and death, every one of us—ministers included—needs the fellowship of a counselor or confessor.

The pastor's task in counseling draws people to him who have normal problems or anxieties; and it also draws those who have mental and emotional illnesses which are deeper than he can treat. These psychological problems concern the pastor as surely as do the *spiritual* problems of his flock. Fortunately, there are allies upon whom we can count today. The skills of the psychologist and psychiatrist are increasing both in depth and extent. While the pastor is neither a psychologist nor a psychiatrist, he should be informed enough about these professions to know when he has reached his own limits and when more competent help is needed for his parishioners. His greatest usefulness to some of his members will be when he guides them to this competent help. I have found that the confessional fellowship with communicants is often a bridge over which persons are led to larger resources and more capable and skillful professionals.

Unhappily, there is not nearly enough team work among psychologists, psychiatrists, and clergymen. Although the old antagonisms are slowly giving way, the advance is not yet rapid enough and broad enough. Perhaps this is due to a lack of understanding, a lack of mutual respect, a distrust which exists in both groups. The unfamiliarity of strange terminology has added to the difficulties. Psychologists know and use our terms of love, hostility, fear, freedom, hate, guilt, but they use them with somewhat different connotations or meanings. Their technical terminology of "id," "ego," "superego," or "cathexes" is a foreign language to us.

The problem is deeper than one of communication, however. It cannot be completely solved until we solve the problem of communication between ministers, rabbis and priests on one hand, and the psychologists and psychiatrists on the other. Furthermore, psychiatry is a newly emerging profession, and all new professions tend to become defensive until they are fully established. When a great Eastern university instituted a new doctorate degree back in the mid-thirties, the majority of those who took the course were automatically held back for a few years to give the degree a reputation, and as a warning to others that this degree was not an easy one to come by.

I find it difficult to say which of us is the more guilty at this juncture. Actually, all of us are trying to help man—man, as an individual—in both physical and spiritual terms. Both minister and psychiatrist attempt to heal him, not as a duality, but as a single entity. Our work, when viewed from this perspective, is complementary. Ministers need more depth in the knowledge of the psychological make-up of human beings, and psychiatrists need more depth in understanding the nature and working of religion, and, perhaps, more contact with the right kind of religion.

I worked for three years in a joint effort with a psychiatrist, Dr. H. Peter Laqueur, in which we dealt with the whole personality of people who needed both of our skills. We usually saw our clients once a week, separately at first, and then together, as needed. In every case we compared notes, but in medical matters Dr. Laqueur's decisions for therapy took precedence over any recommendations of mine. While on occasion we felt that we had not really helped some of the persons who came to us, the overall success of our work was so great that without any publicity we had many times more people asking our aid than we could possibly serve.

Before undertaking our joint effort, we spent nearly four months studying together, trying to understand the areas of our agreements and disagreements, working out methods and techniques, defining terminology of psychiatry and religion, and examining our professions. The experience was one of the most rewarding I have ever had. I think our long weeks of study and preparation together accounted for what success we had. Needless to say, we did not always agree. Yet this did not trouble me, for I have found that the areas of disagreement are considerable between psychiatrists themselves—just as they are between clergymen. The important thing was that we recognized ourselves as partners in the healing of man's mind and soul.

Joshua Loth Liebman, after a full discussion of the areas where the roles of psychiatry and religion complement each other, climaxes the discussion in his book *Peace of Mind* with these words:

> Far from being antagonistic, religion and psychiatry are mutually supplementary. Each is capable of supporting man at points where the other is weakest or has failed. There is no danger that psychiatry will replace religion, nor is it any longer possible for religion to sweep back the rising tide of psychological knowledge that is floating man off the submerged ledges of grief and perplexity. Harried mankind needs both religion and psychiatry. Men should no longer deny themselves the assistance to be derived either from the revealed word of God or the findings of "revealed psychology." Only in the right confluence of these two tides shall we find peace of mind . . .
>
> A religion that will joyously welcome the gifts of modern psychology will be able to deal with human evil in terms of change and creation, will know the darkness of human nature, but will not be dismayed by it, will be

neither naive about human goodness nor pessimistic about human power. Such a religion will be able not merely to describe the good life and its great goals but also to implement that life with indispensable means. Aided by the tools of dynamic psychology, religion will be able to understand far more subtly and profoundly why men hate rather than love, why men grow afraid, surrender to morbidity, and turn in bitterness against the power greater than man. At the same time, this wiser religion will be able to show men and women how to achieve a freer conscience, a less counterfeit love, a more integrated courage, and an undistorted life—affirming communion with God.[10]

Pastoral counseling is bringing people into fellowship with Christ, the Christian fellowship, and fellowship with the pastor as God's agent. It helps them to help themselves by getting a clearer insight into their inner conflicts; it aids them to acknowledge their guilt and to repent of their sins; and it seeks to enable them to live securely with themselves, and in friendship with their brothers. Further, it shows them the way to act out the drama of their lives in confidence. As the shepherd of Christ's fellowship, the pastor has a relationship to persons which is unique in the framework of our society.

In no other profession are so many confidences given so freely, so intimately, and so hopefully. In our experience at the Church of the Master, we found, however, that our parishioners gravitated naturally, almost exclusively, to the one who preached. No matter how able the non-preaching ministers in a Protestant church may be, they are often forced to sit on the sidelines, helpless to help. A breakthrough of confidence from a parishioner to a non-preaching "assistant" is rare. We have, therefore, rotated our preaching schedule in a way that allows each of us to preach about one-third of the time. It helps mightily in relating the people to all of the pastors. We suspect it would also work in other churches.

In the role of pastoral counselor, the pastor is concerned with immediate anxieties most of all; but he also helps his parishioner search back into the past where the roots of a problem are deepest

—and at the same time look ahead, so that the future may be regarded with greater confidence and enhanced self-knowledge. Helping the parishioner to be aware of the possibilities for growth and development, and above all concerned with motives and purposes, the minister yet has as his chief aim the restoration of spiritual wholeness—what the psychologist calls "integration of the personality." The aim is not to vindicate the preacher's moral philosophy, not even to demonstrate the righteous wrath of God, but rather to help persons secure that inner peace of mind and soul from which true happiness and adjusted personalities are derived.

In her book, *The Inner Life of Man*, Dr. Frances G. Wickes tells of two wonderful, adjusted people who greatly impressed her:

> One was a great physician and scientist, and the other a washerwoman in a frontier town. The dissimilarity lay in circumstances and outer community, in gifts and natural ability. The similarity lay in their attitude toward experience; in their ability to live deeply in whatever came to them; and to see the true drama of life as something not produced by circumstances or fate, but by inner relation of events. In each of them one felt, as a dominant quality, a life wisdom, which while drawn from the daily experience, yet penetrated to the level where the inner being of the spirit was revealed and the moment became a part of the greater reality. In each, the judgment of an act was tempered by a form of charity which, always acknowledging its own limitations, was willing to give to others an understanding that helped them to cast out fear, so that bewildered people could see themselves more clearly, and, through this understanding, accept themselves.[11]

The dangers of inadequate and unskillful counseling are many. It is possible for the pastor to do more harm than good if he has inadequate preparation for the task; if he lacks the knowledge of tested techniques: if he does not provide enough uninterrupted time; if he moves too quickly; if he speaks from a dogmatic position; if he allows the parishioner to become dependent upon him; if to avoid causing pain he refrains from complete honesty with the counselee; if he does not sufficiently understand the emotional tone of the problem; if he tries to reduce the problem to a simple proposition of sin and righteousness, cloaking himself with the appearance of self-righteousness; or if he uses coercion (and spiritual coercion can be harsher and sometimes more devastating than physical coercion). Many a pastor has been more of a stumbling block than stepping-stone to security for people in trouble.

One of the worst things a pastor can do is let a parishioner know that he has been shocked by the recital of some sordid tale of sin and failure. I have a beautiful red leather chair in my study. When someone begins his story, "You have never heard anything as bad as my problem," I gently stop him and say, "Then please sit in that red leather chair on the other side of the desk, because I reserve that seat for the person who has fallen from grace lower than any of my other friends and acquaintances." Then I hasten to tell the story of Jesus and the woman taken in adultery, and my visitor is at ease.

The minister counsels in a fellowship of confession in which Christ's love draws both close to God, for God never lets go and is ever seeking to redeem and win us back to Himself.

But a knowledge of techniques alone is not enough. The preacher has a spiritual reservoir of God's love and compassion upon which to draw. He should develop his art as religiously as a painter develops his skill with the brush, or the doctor his branch of the healing profession. Human agents can go only so far. There comes a time for God, and the minister can help usher the soul he shepherds into the Presence where support and direction can be found. "Man's extremity is God's opportunity" of helping us face up to the inner life.

The chaos of inner confusion is damaging to the personality. The minister helps the parishioner understand and probe that inner life—the life which is not new to any one of us but lies beneath the surface neglected, or—because it is so painful—pushed from the memory. When we are in conflict with the inner life, we are not whole persons—we are, indeed, morally or mentally sick persons. When that inner life is neglected we are not full, adult personalities upon whom either God or society can depend.

III

Ministers are often lonely men, and their need for warm, rewarding personal fellowships is greater than they frequently recognize. The rural preacher in particular must often be alone in soul and spirit, isolated as he is from even his fellow clergymen, and usually without any professional assistants with whom to share his defeats, problems, and triumphs. If this were merely a problem of time and space, it could be more easily solved. But it is a much deeper problem. Even in thickly populated towns and metropolitan centers, relationships between clergymen are often superficial even when both are members of the same denomination. This is the situation; yet confronting us is the knowledge that all pastors have a deep need for a truly confessional relationship— a friendship so sure and firm that it would enable one to share all his thoughts with a brother-confessor. And share them in the same confidence and with the same expectation of understanding that parishioners feel when speaking with their pastor!

There are thoughts, events, problems, defeats, anxieties, and failures which ministers cannot discuss even with those laymen with whom they have the closest personal ties. Ever-present are the dangers of misinterpretation or misrepresentation—either sufficient to impair the pastor-communicant relationship, and adulterate the pastor's effectiveness.

In other words, there is a large area in which he cannot "let his hair down," to use a commonly understood phrase, without risking serious limitations to his ministry. And when he cannot readily do this even with one of his fellow clergy, his frustrations only deepen and his anxieties increase. Ministers can share their joys and triumphs with most people. They can seldom share their defeats and personal failures with anyone.

Moreover, every pastor carries in his heart and mind the heavy burdens of many of his communicants who have given him their confidences. Many of these confidences and vexing problems he dare not discuss even with his wife. While members of the congregation often act in other matters as though they had called the minister's wife, too, when they employed him, they rightfully expect that the pastor—and not his wife—is the repository of their innermost secrets. There would be few, indeed, who would go to their pastor and honestly unburden themselves if they did not believe that his promise of confidence was unassailable.

There are times when a pastor's wife is not as wise as she might be. Should she come into conflict with a person whose confidence her husband has shared with her, she may not be able to keep reason and objectivity in control of her emotions. It takes a wise, loving, and deeply devoted wife, one who is not easily hurt, to understand the pastor's delicate relationship to members of the flock. Multiplying the problem is the fact that people usually expect more of her than they have a right to. If she moves forward too fast, they are apt to be hyper-critical of her actions. She is especially vulnerable when dissident individuals and groups in the church are hostile to her husband. People often "get at" her husband by abusing her. When problems, inadvertently or otherwise, arise around his wife, the pastor's burdens are greatly increased. Should her marriage relationship with her husband reach a crisis stage, she is the only member of the church who is without a pastor. Unless they both agree to it, she cannot go to one of her husband's fellow ministers for comfort or spiritual advice, without further enlarging the area of conflict.

Thus it is that few men in any other professions carry such crushing emotional burdens as ministers. In a single day, a pastor may have to sit through one or more extremely delicate personal problems. For example, he may visit an incurable patient—and it may be his task to explain what neither the doctor nor the family has disclosed: how slim are the patient's chances of recovery. He may be called upon to give advice to a distraught woman made miserable by a shaky marriage. Her husband stub-

bornly refuses even to discuss the problem with the pastor—
while the mate who *does* consult him has nevertheless, in her
anxiety, done all the wrong things.

Or the pastor may seek to establish a relationship of confidence
with some member of his flock whom he sees falling into serious
error. He wishes to be able to initiate discussion on a positive
and constructive basis—which is more easily said than done if
the person either consciously or unconsciously avoids him.

Or he may have to counsel with an elderly person who is un-
loved and unwanted by his family and shoved aside by time and
society, yet who still desperately desires to remain independent,
despite ineligibility for social security benefits, despite lack of
savings, despite inability to work.

Nor is the pastor's burden lightened by the fact that many a
person who isn't sufficiently integrated to make his own decisions
therefore looks to the minister to make them for him.

Any one of these problems would be sufficient to weight the
minister down—yes, just one of these, without the additional
problems of church organization, administration, and finance which
daily assail him. And then even beyond these trials of his mind
and soul are the grievous conditions of society and the world,
causing deep concern and pressing in on every side in these
times of trouble and change.

With all this as much a part of him as blood and breath, it is easy
to see why there are times when the minister may come to
believe that he is a better man, a more capable worker than he
really is. And more—the very fact that he is a minister, a man
who should have a special aptitude for insight and discernment,
is likely to increase his resistance both to self-examination and the
cathartic of talking with a brother confessor. Many a preacher
expounds upon the theme of "facing up to life" in his sermons,
but does not face up to it himself.

That ministers are not infallible is readily admitted by clergymen themselves. They are psychological beings, capable of both
the lowest and highest levels of human living. Our Lord Jesus
said, "There is none perfect but the Father." Their egos can be so

inflated by pride, vanity, and desire for prestige that humility becomes a mere word to use to others.

Ministers often get into serious difficulties, breach some of the laws which they must ever uphold, fail to achieve maturity, become dogmatic and inflexible and confused as to the purpose of their calling, get embroiled in avoidable difficulties with their congregations, wallow in antagonistic controversies with brother clergyman—and sometimes, in the intensity of all this, lose sight of the love and brotherhood they proclaim. (Their temptations are so many that it is amazing they succumb so infrequently!)

It is not easy for the minister to see himself as a sinner in constant need of heaven's mercy and grace precisely because, even though a sinner, he is, paradoxically, a part of the divine plan of salvation to help lead others from sin to righteousness. Ministers need constant vigilance to escape the all too easily acquired sin of intentional self-righteousness. The New Testament witness had ministers as well as laymen in mind when he said, "If we say that we have no sin, we deceive ourselves, and the truth is not in us. If we confess our sins, he is faithful and just to forgive us our sins and to cleanse us from all unrighteousness." (I JOHN 1:8-9)

Then why do we not confess our sins and our needs to our brothers in the ministry? Why in this area is the gap so very wide between our teachings and our actions?

The reasons are not hard to discover. First of all there are psychological "resistances" to honest, free uncovering and unburdening of ourselves and our inner lives, even to one whom we trust. Second, our pride is a barrier—especially our pride as ministers. Are we not ministers who should be able to handle our own problems? Do we not tell others how to deal with theirs? Have we not also been ordained to the gospel ministry? Will we lose prestige with our brother minister if we reveal our innermost secrets? These are real questions, considering what we know of ourselves and often think about our fellow ministers.

Third, are we afraid that our confidence may not be kept? This in itself is a serious indictment of some in the clergy: do our parishioners also fear this when they come to us in their troubles? Do they—and we—fear that our brother may inadvertently reveal our secret by careless illustration in a talk or a sermon?

Added to these are the fears that our position among the clergy may be seriously handicapped if we disclose personal conflicts—that such "knowledge" about us will curb our chances of advancement in our denomination.

Finally, divisions resulting from a feeling of competition, or growing out of differing theological concepts, are apt to create very difficult emotional barriers, not at all conducive to the development of a confessional fellowship between preachers.

What is needed among clergy is a brother confessor relationship of great competence, spiritual maturity, balance, humility, and love for men, the world, and for the kingdom. There are some areas—and this is one of them—where ministers need the fellowship of confession. A brother confessor who has been through the deep waters of travail in his own soul, and having grown in the spirit as a result, can say, "I am on the bottom, brother, and it feels mighty good," Such a man can be of inestimable help to a brother passing through the dark night of his own troubles.

The fellowship of confession of which I speak is something higher than a buddy-relationship between two or more pastors who play golf together. It is a deeper relationship than a Presbytery, Classis, Synod, Ministers' Association, Conference or Diocesan relationship, in which ministers are members by virtue of belonging to the same denominational group. Such relationships are vital to the life of the church as an institution, but are seldom, if ever, deep enough to meet our deepest needs. A confessional fellowship will as often as not cross over denominational lines. In my own case, if I may be permitted a personal example, I have found it in two brothers of the other denominations—one is Episcopalian, and the other Evangelical and Reformed.

The voluntary unburdening of oneself to a brother confessor is, I can tell you, a painful experience. But our hours together—in confession, advice, and prayer—became a fellowship of both agony and hope. Neither of my two friends sat in judgment, but through the graciousness of their understanding I was brought face to face with God's judgment, and through them I perhaps first really experienced the power of forgiveness, and the assurance of their help and of God's untiring support once I was willing in humility to accept His high demands for my life. I did not find this easy—but I did find it an experience which was profoundly cleansing and spiritually strengthening. The love of my brother confessors for me was manifest in their continued and full acceptance of me in confidence as a fellow clergyman.

Until we have this experience ourselves, we can never fully appreciate how painfully difficult it is for people to articulate their distress in utter honesty. God alone knows the time it takes to achieve adequate self-knowledge so that one may touch that redemption which makes whole again, and only God knows the many subterfuges and disguises our conscience often wears. I am convinced that exploring our soul with a brother confessor is a deeply rewarding experience of great spiritual intensity, much like "a thoughtful woman who uses two mirrors," as someone once said, "to get a double reflection, one which she holds up before her face, and one behind her head."

We may not agree with all the aspects of confession as the Roman Catholic Church practices it, but there is, nevertheless, much in it of great merit. We dislike some of the compulsion and penalties; we are uneasy at the abuses and escapes to which many Catholics put it, yet it is true that we never really face ourselves until we face our own consciences in the mirror of a trusted brother's confidence and love. We know that he cannot absolve us, but on the other hand we also know that he can indeed help draw us closer to the necessary purgation, that he can enable us to clear away the self-deception and the encrusted debris which saps our spiritual strength.

The expression, "self-confession is good for the soul," is more than a trite phrase; it is an unconscious witness to a deeply felt human need. All men and women know the urgent need on many occasions to pour out their tragedies, failures, and fears to someone who loves them and deeply cares. The lost religious therapy of confession needs to be revived among evangelicals. The Apostle James admonishes all Christian brethren to "Confess your faults one to another and pray one for another, that ye may be healed." (JAMES 5:16) Confession is not to be taken or dismissed lightly. It is a holy thing. It must have its safeguards and it should always be done in privacy, to those loving and holy enough to share fully the experience. The very act of entering into the fellowship of a Christian church demands confession first to God and then confession to a group of Christians into whose fellowship the seeker desires admission. St. Paul writing to the Christians at Rome said, "For with the heart man believeth unto righteousness; and with the mouth confession is made unto salvation." (ROMANS 10:10)

Those pastors who stood firm for the faith, who literally held the church together when Adolf Hitler—at the height of his power and popularity—tried to stamp out religious opposition, were members of what they secretly called a "confessional brotherhood." They met in hidden places, used a language of signs and symbols, and were seldom a jump ahead of Hitler's secret police. A great many of them were thrown into prison and many others lost their lives. The secret of their strength and the power of their witness was sustained and drawn from their confessional brotherhood. They had to be absolutely and openly honest, dependent, confidential and frank with each other. Each had to be humble enough to be advised, supported, and disciplined by another.

Such wisdom, strength and spiritual power does not need a crisis to be realized. We, each of us, can realize it here and now. It can be of such spiritual depth—it can rise to such victorious heights of Christian love—that in confidence we can drop our pretensions and reservations, and see ourselves as we are!

The trinity of confessional fellowships in which the minister stands is inextricably interwoven between God, man, and ourselves. A deepened and vital fellowship with God provides the spiritual awareness and the wisdom for those who grow into that fellowship, through us. It establishes the conditions of love, and the true humility of the confessional relationship, of which we are the recipients in the hour of our need. We dare not set a standard of preference which demands one set of procedures and methods for the communicants, and another for ourselves. The lack of a positive fellowship of confession presents Protestant clergy with one of the greatest challenges of our time. Through lack of it, many a minister, by evading and covering his personal defeats and failures with a veneer of religious respectability and piety, has failed to be the mighty witness for God he could have been. If some of us had not been such miserable stumbling blocks on the highways to the Kingdom, many more souls might have gotten in. When we find that great commitment which prepares the way for the whole-hearted surrender of self which is necessary to insure moral and spiritual victory, then God is fashioning us for tremendous usefulness in His service.

III

PREACHING TO
MEN OR MORTAR

THE vast *general* becomes the narrow *particular* to every clergyman, the two fusing inescapably when our task is well done. The nation becomes the city, the city becomes the parish to the man who is faced with the problems of guiding an urban flock. The city church is a microcosm of society, yet its specific character sets it apart from country churches or small town churches.

The *New York Daily News*, proudly glorifying the constant change and spreading growth of America's largest metropolis, carries a page of picture contrasts each Sunday under the head-line, "New York's Changing Scene." These intimate glimpses of a complex, sprawling city startle our imagination and increase our wonder at the creative genius of man. But the story is always about business enterprises, subways, industry, piers, loading cranes and harbors, areas of amusement, the garment district, Coney Island and Broadway, building and expansion of educational institutions, churches, cathedrals, and synagogues—almost as though they went up by themselves, without being in themselves the creative expression of the genius of man to meet the increased hunger of men and the needs of men.

True to our time, the emphasis is placed upon the mortar which binds the stones together, interlaces the streets, and thrusts up the towers of modern buildings. Man, made in the image of God, is lost in the shadow of the buildings and the caverns of the streets. To a greater extent than we perhaps know, man—for whom, Jesus said, the Sabbath exists—finds himself measured by material things and not really as "valuable" or as "important" as steel, stone, brick, and mortar. Man, for whom God made the world, increasingly finds himself cast in the role of an economic and material being—a slave, so to speak, with only pretensions of dignity and illusions of freedom. Bernice Rodgers, Deputy Commissioner of Buildings and Housing of the City of New York, is neither a preacher nor a religious leader, but she has reminded us that "housing is people—not stones and brick and mortar."

There is nothing unusual about the *Daily News* idea, for it is duplicated by the Chambers of Commerce and the newspapers of every city from Boston to San Diego, from Seattle to Key West; it is a part of the mad race to idolize material bigness. It is part of the pride of being first in something different; it is expressed in a conceit and shallowness which make it necessary to out-boast about everything. Nor does it matter much what that *everything* is. The temptation reaches the point where the expert in civic planning and the public relations' advocate of civic pride even apologize for the rain in certain sunny areas—although man has not yet found another way to get water into the ground.

Publications, both religious and secular, glorify our modern achievements, and tell us reams about buildings and things, but very little about people—people who give the areas and the institutions life, personality, and character, and without whom nothing material has any meaning whatsoever. There is no hint at all, in the pictures, of the drama of life which flows around the scenes, sometimes serenely and sometimes turbulently. There is no hint of the doctor who comes at midnight in response to the urgency of a life teetering at the portals of death's dark door, of the happiness at a wedding when a new home is being formed, or the tragedy of a wayward son in conflict with his parents, or the sad emptiness of a broken home, or the courage of a policeman who gives his life in the line of sworn duty to protect the innocent and the unwary, or of the great festivals of faith where the preacher's love mends the ladder of God's grace and helps to lift the souls of men above the chasms of despair where their bodies are trapped.

I once heard an eminent New York pastor say in jest—although he disclaimed authorship for the statement—"Every preacher has two prayers: 'Lord, let me go to heaven when I die; but please give me a New York church *before* I die.' " There is an element of profound truth in the sentiment, for the modern city has opportunities for the preaching of the gospel which have no equal. Within a stone's throw of any city church—a distance no farther than Alexander the Great's throw across the Indus River—are hundreds of lost souls almost untouched by the preaching of the ministers.

The city has had a fascination for men as far back as recorded history can reach. Men fled to it as a refuge from persecution and loneliness. They sought the safety of its walls when invasion threatened, but they sought it more often because it was a busy, bustling place where money could be made, where there were fewer restraints than in small places. Romance, excitement, and bright lights stimulated their imagination, accelerated their coming, and delayed their departure. City dwellers like to live "where things happen"—but without being too deeply involved, and without being committed to responsibilities. As Murray H. Leiffer wrote in his book, *The Effective City Church:*

> The city has always drawn to itself the most diverse
> personalities. The prophet goes there to secure an au-
> dience and to preach against urban vices; the prostitute
> flees to it in order to escape the criticism of her towns-
> people; the genius and the eccentric find companion-
> ship with people like themselves; and thrill-seeking

youth look for excitement and adventure. However, the vast majority of city dwellers are neither illustrious saints nor profligate sinners. They are the run-of-the-mill men and women seeking to improve their economic status and hoping to give their children more opportunities than they themselves enjoyed in their youth. They, like the others, find in the city diversity and richness of experience in human association which are not easily procurable in the small town or the open country.[1]

One of man's greatest achievements, the city is, by the same token, his curse. It is a necessary concomitant of our industrial and mechanical civilization, enticing thousands of hopeful men and women in search of a more secure and happy life. It plays upon man's gregarious instincts and draws him within its boundaries, ensnares him with its shimmering illusions of grandeur, whets his appetite for more and more tangible evidence of material wealth, and then with its noise, dirt, filth, its decadent neighborhoods and impersonalizations, it drives him away.

But even then, he lingers in the suburbs, incapable of breaking the magic spell of the city, desirous of taking advantage of its benefits of art, music, and culture, hopeful of exploiting its economic resources for personal security and gain without too much responsibility for its maintenance, or involvement in its immense and complex problems. Thousands, unable to escape the greedy grasp of its mechanical tentacles, forage as best they can for some residue of decency, happiness, and security.

Most people would be better off in smaller towns and cities, for large cities inevitably tend to depersonalize and to cheapen the lives of their inhabitants. Problems arise which are almost too gigantic and complex to be coped with successfully. Indifference breeds calloused vulgarity; proximity steals away pride and sensitivity; many of the cities' school children do not receive a full day's schooling because "short shifts" are necessary to accommodate the numbers of children, and of those who do get the full day in school, nearly half are in classes far too large for good educational practice.

Every city has almost insoluble tax problems. Some of our cities have grown to the point where their problems are impossible of solution. It would be best to break them up, but on the contrary the influx continues faster than the suburbs draw them off. Robinson Jeffers dramatized our plight in the city with a flash of insight in the fourth stanza of his poem *Shine, Perishing Republic,* when he wrote:

> But for my children, I would have them keep their distance
>   from the thickening center; corruption
> Never has been compulsory, when the cities lie at the
>   monster's feet there are left the mountains.[2]

But industry and commerce are the life of the city and the foundation of the nation's economy. Without them, men could not have bread. Industry and commerce create a concentrated population which crowds itself into houses which men would not voluntarily choose—houses built to accommodate a half or a third less of humanity.

Individuals are lost in this kind of crowd. And there is no loneliness anywhere equal to the loneliness of a man lost in the crowd at Times Square, the Loop, or Wilshire Boulevard. There is more extensive hunger in the midst of the city's plenty than anywhere else in our society—hunger in a deeper sense than hunger for food, since welfare agencies of no modern city ever let anyone starve. It is the hunger for privacy and peace of mind, needed by a man if he is to keep counsel with his soul and maintain his sanity and his dignity. It is the hunger for friends—friends to whom he is important, not mere associates and acquaintances thrust upon him by a proximity he cannot escape. It is hunger for the quiet respite from noise at hours other than those reserved for sleep. His hunger for the night silence when he "knits up the ravelled sleeve of care" in the hope that, tomorrow, he may have the strength and wisdom to find a way out of the city's maze. Alas, this tomorrow never comes for most of those pinioned by the machines of industry.

Long before the powerful pressures of the city metamorphosed residential neighborhoods into miserable, all-too-prevalent slums, many preachers were preaching to empty pews enshrined in mortar and stone. Churches, built to last a hundred years in new communities, found the problems they had sought to escape leapfrogging after them in twenty-five to forty years. A great mass of new citizens "invaded the area" (to use a sociologically correct but most inappropriate phrase), and the church builders had to face the same problems all over again, almost before they had paid off the debt on the property. We found ourselves trapped by the identification of a church with a building: mortar become more precious than men. And like the Levites, we passed thousands on the very doorsteps of the church.

The city draws men together, but it so accentuates the dilemma of their diversities that the church finds its functions confused, and the preacher finds his role distorted. Both congregations and pastors are baffled by the shifting communities of a changing city. It is a harsh commentary upon the city church that political parties, labor unions, lodges, and social clubs are often more successful in welding men of wide differences into a unity for a common purpose than is a temple of God. And it is a bitter commentary on the preacher that the politician and the labor leader are more persuasive in winning the loyalty of all manner of men to their organization than we are in winning men to our religious institutions.

The flight is away from the city church to the suburbs. Such has been the case for a long time, with the crucial stage reached in the last two decades. Today, according to a report published in December, 1954, by the Regional Planning Association (with headquarters in New York City), the flight is not only from the cities to suburban areas, but even more so to suburban suburbia— "exurbia." There may have been a time when the church either preceded the community or was there at the birth of the new neighborhood, but that time is now past. Today the church follows the community. This pattern has obtained for the past five decades. The church now follows its congregation, if the congregation can pay, and this procedure will doubtless continue.

No one will deny the fineness and loyalty of people who, for the love of God, sacrifice to build a new church. But when the congregation moves, many are left behind who also need the love of God, the guidance of the church, and the care of the shepherds of Christ's flock. And nearly always, two or three times more people are left in the midst of these deteriorating neighborhoods than were there when the original congregation and pastor first built the house of worship.

The greatest irony is that many of these fugitive churches never achieved the hope of Jesus: "My house shall be a house of prayer for all people." Many failed in their neighborhood because they sought out only the like-minded and the people of similar racial and national backgrounds. As though an excluding church could ever be one of the churches of our Lord Jesus Christ!

Obviously the church must serve its entire neighborhood. If the neighborhood served is of one race and one economic group —all well and good. But this is seldom the case in a complex, modern city. Nevertheless, we continue to seek the parishioners of our particular flock even when they have scattered over the city, far beyond our reach, and we carry their names on our rolls long after their tenuous membership has ceased to have validity, although the unlike in race, national origin, class, and culture, are so near that we could reach out and claim them without even the aid of a shepherd's crook.

It would be adventurous preaching of great merit to encourage the congregation to break down the "middle-wall of partition" when the constituency of the neighborhood changes. And of even greater merit to preach so clearly and minister so inclusively as to lead them in.

Because of our unwillingness to preach the full gospel of oneness in the body of Christ, and because of man's pride of difference and his sin of natural divisiveness, we have not succeeded in bringing together men of various races, nations, classes, and cultures as one family in God, conscious of their common origin and destiny. Few indeed are there among the clergy who have not at some time quoted St. Paul on there being neither Jew nor Greek, bond nor free, barbarian nor Scythian in Christ Jesus—but fewer are those who have the courage to stand up and be counted for this ideal.

The serious problems of the city church are born of the perplexing problems of the city itself, which are always in transition. To lay them solely at the door of congregations or pastors—although they do not escape complicity to the degree that they fail to understand and to relate themselves positively to urban problems—would be an oversimplification of community dynamics. The church as an institution does not exist in a vacuum. Mobility—a factor over which the church has no control—is an ever-increasing problem. It began first with the drift from the primary relationships of the towns, finally culminating in the amorphous group life of the city. It was further stimulated by the waves of emigration from Europe which involved fundamental changes in culture and in human relationships. It became especially apparent during World War II, when nearly thirty million civilians and Armed Forces' personnel moved restlessly from "pillar to post" because of the exigencies of the military effort. Mobility, in a word, has become part of the character of modern existence—the machine which drives the wheels of industry has seen to that.

We have been a fairly footloose population in America for the last decade and a half. From 1940 to 1947, a relatively brief period, seventy million Americans changed their place of abode at least once. Over twenty-five million of these persons either changed their residences twice, or moved outside the county in which they formerly lived. In the same period, one out of every eight who lived on a farm moved to a small town, a medium sized city or an urban center. The extent of this exaggerated restlessness can be seen by the fact that these amazing movements took place during World War II, when housing was tightest. It takes no great stretch of the imagination to recognize how such mobility affects the life and place of the church, and the damage it does to both the individual and the family's sense of belonging. When men and women, formerly of a rural area or a small town, revisit that place after years in the city, both they and their relatives and their former associates recognize at once how the city has changed personalities.

Even before the advent of the automobile-for-all, organized

religion was having a hard time maintaining the loyalty of church members. As a Roman Catholic priest once sadly remarked, "Scores of my parishioners come to church only twice in their lives, and are carried in both times—for baptism and burial." The same is true for Protestants with two notable modifications: the word *scores* should be multiplied to hundreds, and we should remind ourselves that perhaps many more nominal Christians, who never come to church, are buried from funeral parlors than from churches. A few manage to arrange to be married in the church, even if they are not seen there again until they get into trouble. And many will bring their child for baptism—since the child is then too young to come alone. (Lest we grow hopeful, remember that these same parents will manage to send that child off to Sunday school alone a few years later!) Does this mean they are gone from us, irretrievably? No, because these same people—impelled by earlier training or a vague desire for inner security and escape from frustration, worries, and disturbances—are apt to overflow the churches on Easter, Christmas, and New Year's Eve.

While neither the minister nor the church can be wholly blamed for this loss of loyalty, the more thoughtful leaders of the church earnestly hope that we will one day find both the message and the method to help these people to a satisfying faith and a fellowship which will bind them to the church. So far, we have been frustrated by the evil genius of the city.

Individuals on the move fail to identify themselves with institutions, and families changing their residences from one community to another have a difficult time acquiring a real sense of belonging. Children are unable to develop close primary ties, the products of a settled community life. The easy payment plan has brought Ezekiel's "wheel within a wheel," in the form of the automobile, within the reach of moderate wage earners; persistent and attractive advertising has broken the resistance of those who can afford this modern means of transportation only at the sacrifice of more elemental necessities. Thus Sunday becomes perhaps the most mobile day of the week, when those who cannot otherwise escape the claustrophobia of the city find momentary relief in the country or at the beach. This may be hard on church attendance, but it is certainly a blessing—in one sense at least—to those whose lives are poured into the crucible of hectic city existence.

Nor do small towns and medium-sized cities lying in close proximity to urban cities, or those towns which are constantly springing up around large industries, escape the vitiating process of mobility-on-wheels.

When members of any local church, then, cease to be concerned about the survival of the church and the welfare of the community, wholesome existence is seriously threatened. And when a sizeable segment of the community puts its own economic interests, its own pleasures, or even its own religious well-being above the welfare of the area of which it is an integral part, a collapse of major proportions is imminent. Social metabolism is constantly at work in a city. This is the price we must pay—perhaps an all-too-costly one—for the measure of the progress we demand. Religious institutions, of necessity, have to take these facts into consideration as they plan their programs. Under the circumstances the preacher's task needs constant re-evaluation.

Children and youth are among the first and highest price society pays when building its economy and expanding its cities. Juvenile delinquency is largely a product of urbanization. That this is true may be plainly seen when we look away from our scene to Africa, where new urban centers have evolved only in the last two or three decades. Juvenile delinquency, a phenomenon unknown in African tribal society, has now risen to major proportions in the new cities.

But one doesn't have to look beyond the borders of the nation into mission lands to find the ever-changing problems which arise out of urbanization. Changing patterns of all kinds abound in our city on the very door step of almost every church.

We have had to reckon with the perplexities of changing city patterns and problems at the Church of the Master, which is located on the western border of the Harlem area of New York City. In the short space of one decade, the racial complexion, economic level, and cultural pattern and social structure went through three distinctive changes. In the beginning the immediate neighborhood surrounding the church was a fourth American Negro with a sprinkling of West Indian, a fourth white Protestant, forty percent Irish Catholic and ten percent Jewish. Within five years the proportions had changed to fifty percent Negro, ten percent white Protestant, twenty percent Irish and five percent Jewish. The remaining fifteen percent of the population was an entirely new group. They were Puerto Ricans. Before the next five years had passed, the Jews and white Protestants had moved, and the Irish population had been reduced to less than ten percent, while the Negro population had expanded to sixty-five percent and our Puerto Rican friends had grown to twenty-five percent.

During this period, changing patterns of cultural outlook, welfare necessities, unemployment, over-crowded housing, juvenile delinquency, disintegration of family life and group conflicts, largely between teen-agers, closely followed the shifts in population. The ministers and the officers of the Church of the Master geared their religious concern and social outreach to meet the needs occasioned by these changes. One result of their efforts was the establishment of the Morningside Community Center, a social service and welfare program under religious auspices for all the groups of the community. Since the church is located in juxtaposition to the Morningside Heights section of New York, the church involved students and faculty of the Union Theological Seminary, Teachers and Barnard Colleges of Columbia University and the College of the City of New York in the development and extension of its program.

Demolition of old housing and the erection of two gigantic housing projects for middle and low income families forecast a new cycle of change. Although the end result of these changes is not yet clearly seen, the ministers, officers and members of the Church of the Master are already at work preparing the machinery and program for the necessary adjustment. Readjustments in church program and emphasis to meet neighborhood changes are very difficult, but the rewards are worth all the upheavals and trials of the minds and souls of the clergy and their flock.

When a church refuses to recognize the nature of community growth and change, or when preachers close their minds to the necessity of interpreting the change in the light of the eternal truth, they not only intensify the problem but jeopardize their right to existence and the power of their witness. The process of inevitable adjustment is rendered more acute by denying the necessity for change—unless ignoring the facts of the situation, or running away, are considered "adjustment." This conservatism, with which preachers have had large experience, arises out of the unconscious response to habit patterns deeply imbedded in the psychology of all human beings. Thomas Jefferson wrote, ". . . all experience has shown that mankind are more disposed to suffer while evils are sufferable, than to right themselves by abolishing the forms to which they are accustomed." By stubbornly refusing to change (or even admit to the necessity for change), some religious people unwittingly heap problems upon an already chaotic situation.

There were no modern cities as complex as ours in the day when Jesus lived, but there were cities deeply stained with sin. Cities are a conglomeration of men, and men are sinners until redeemed by the grace of God. Jerusalem even today has not changed much—except that like Berlin it is now a divided city, rent by two implacable forces face to face across a barrier as thin as a strand of wire, but as wide and deep as the hatred and antagonisms of sinful men can make it.

When our Lord lamented, "Jerusalem, Jerusalem . . . how often would I have gathered thy children together, even as a hen gathereth her chickens under her wings, and ye would not," he was troubled with the misery of its poor, huddled in hovels. He was troubled by its hunger for bread, friendship, and love. For Jerusalem the Golden had its share of poverty, its heartaches, its lost men and women, its dens of vice and wickedness, its charlatans and exploiters, its temples isolated from the seekers after God. Jerusalem had its men of power, pride, and prestige, who protected their profits by killing the prophets. And it even had its priests who shared the house of prayer with thieves and money changers, men who used devices similar to those many of our city churches use today in order to keep their doors open in these chaotic times. Jerusalem had its prejudices too. Cultural, racial, religious, and political differences were open sores oozing the venom of spite and treachery between Pharisee and Sadducee, Zealots and Essenes, Herodians, Romans, and Samaritans. This was enough to break the heart of God and the body of Jesus on a rough-hewn cross!

We can well imagine, if we only would, what scathing words mingled with pity would fall from our Lord's lips if he viewed the cities man has made and saw the mess these cities have created in men's lives and his Church. If he stood high on the Wrigley Building in Chicago, between the Gold Coast Outer Drive and the sorrowful slums of the Southside, or on the RCA Building in New York, the vantage point from which to survey the intense poverty of Harlem and the squalor of the waterfront, where the tides of labor conflict flow as ceaselessly as the water that floats majestic ocean liners, or on the Cadillac Building in downtown Detroit, surrounded by endless miles of factories which help to make the nation mobile, but which also make the laborer a prisoner to the tedious monotony of ingenious machines—then Jesus would see the desperate complex of modern society lying before him. And his gaze could not escape Paradise Valley—a name given to a neighborhood of degradation and destitution because our uneasy conscience attempts to evoke laughter to cover up sordidness and sorrow.

Our cities are much like Jerusalem, for Jerusalem is a noble city of historic eminence where the eager feet of pilgrims have for untold centuries been turning to pay homage to God's quest for man. Its fabulous wealth has been described in the pages of history. Its beautiful buildings, temples and gardens justified the title of the hymn, *Jerusalem the Golden*. I once saw its golden domes glistening in the late afternoon sun as I stood near the edge of the Dead Sea nearly twenty miles away and twelve hundred feet below it. Rich in the lore of poets, musicians, philosophers, and theologians, it was a prize sought after by the Crusaders, and is still fought over today by a revived Israel and the modern Amonites whose headquarters remain, in spite of time and change, at the old site of Biblical days. It was the city of man's dreams. That is why Jesus wept over it. It held so much promise, but achieved such meager realization of that promise.

Our cities are achievements to inspire the same poetic language of praise and adoration. They are more modern and more efficient; they have more sumptuous edifices of culture, education, and religion—and most of them have a larger population than Jerusalem can ever hope to have. There is much in them to commend to the best in man, and even to the hope of God. We can be justly proud of their materialistic grandeur. Yet Jesus wept over Jerusalem, and we can weep over our cities which promise so much goodness and realize so little of that goodness. In every one of our cities, churches are either making an insignificant impression upon the problems of sin and evil, or are seeking the first opportunity of flight to a more favorable environment—depending upon their individual definitions of the word favorable. It is a flight from mounting problems almost too complex and immense for the city fathers to cope with successfully, and meanwhile the sheep are left wandering without sufficient shepherds.

There is no need to name a particular city. Any city on earth will do. One may take his choice, for they all have manmade hills and are guilty of the same conditions against which Jesus pronounced God's judgment.

The problem of the city church is a problem of the culture and the economy of our time. Racial animosities play a large part. One city differs from another only in the degree and intensity of its racio-religious problems. In one area it may be represented by the Japanese, in another by the Mexican, in another by poor southern whites who have moved north and brought intense prejudices into complacent communities. In almost all cases there is also the leaven of the Negro who is constantly expanding as his standard of living inches upward.

A minister in Chicago, where I was serving as consultant on city church problems, asked me, "When do you think this problem will end? Where will it stop? We got settled one place and then, behold, the next thing we know, Negroes are moving into the new neighborhood." I suggested that there is no end to the problem and that eventually the preachers and the churches will have to make up their minds to stop running, and face it.

When a layman on Long Island asked me a similar question, I suggested that he might save himself trouble if he moved a hundred miles out to the end of the Island, for the movement of Negroes to better communities is an indication of national prosperity, and it will last as long as the nation's economy continues to improve. My friend would, indeed, be better off on the very brink of the ocean's edge, because then he would have no other place to move but to sea, like Lieutenant Noland. Unless, that is, he could learn to live as a Christian with his neighbors, as he should have done in the first place. Until and unless we live up to the high demands of our Christ, we must face the woes of his eternal judgment:

> Woe unto you, scribes and Pharisees, hypocrites! for ye shut up the kingdom of heaven against men: for ye neither go in yourselves, neither suffer ye them that are entering to go in. (St. Matthew 23:13)

> Woe unto you, scribes and Pharisees, hypocrites! for ye pay tithe of mint and anise and cummin, and have omitted the weightier matters of the law, judgment, mercy, and faith; these ought ye to have done, and not to leave the others undone. (St. Matthew 23:23)

The same gross injustices are prevalent everywhere. The same discrimination, indifference, and easy virtues march boldly along with the self-righteous. The same poverty exists in the midst of the greatest prosperity of our history. We raise and give large sums for charity, yet men in high places will not give surplus goods to the hungry. The religious institutions are in a similar position. Many of them—beautiful pieces of architecture—are empty; some of them operate with a handful of proud resisters to time and change —even to God—as does a church in New York which put down a costly carpet for its handful of attendants, but makes no effort to reach out to scores of thousands who remain unchurched in the immediately surrounding area.

We ministers are preoccupied with the operation of the physical plant. Nearly a fourth of our funds goes annually into building improvements and expansion. On the surface, this seems natural enough—we are behind in building needs. But much of our building is unnecessary, and some of it merely ornamentation and duplication. There is little or no renovation of old or construction of new churches in the crowded areas where life is precarious and religious needs staggering. And missions, faced with a magnificent challenge in Asia, and the opportunity of the century in Africa, can scarcely get sufficient funds to undertake minimum activities.

Jesus would rightly ask us, "Which is more important—souls or buildings? men or mortar?" And the reply of most of us would make him weep.

What must the Church do? What must the preacher say? How are we to save our cities and Christ's Church and ourselves? Weep? No—weeping is only the beginning of contrition! Jesus wept, but he did more than that.

He moved boldly to cleanse the temple, for contrition leads to action fired by faith in the strong love of eternal God, with Whom all things are possible. The psalmist has written, "Except the Lord keep the city, the watchman waketh but in vain." (PSALMS 127:1)

Shall we agree that the destructive forces of urbanization are all evil, and attempt to destroy the city? Or shall we abandon it? Jesus did neither. He knew he could not stop the march of progress. That is neither within our rights nor our might. And he did not run away; he went back into the very heart of its miserable existence. The city was not then, and is not now, all evil—though it often stunts the growth of man's spirit and shrivels his soul. As a matter of fact, it brings many blessings. We could scarcely do without the city. The sin is not in the city. The sin is in the men who inhabit the cities. If men yield themselves up to it, sin becomes their master.

Shall we fear the city, run away from it, and go merrily on our way? Consigning it to oblivion is of no avail, for it is too big to be overlooked and too enticing to be forgotten. Jesus went back into the city again and again. The truth of the matter is that we too must stay in it or come back to it again and again. We have a modern example before us in Cincinnati, Ohio, in the Episcopal church of which Charles Taft is a vestryman. After serious study and prayerful consideration, this church made the decision to remain in the heart of its changed neighborhood and face up to its perplexing problems. A vigorous campaign to raise funds to recondition and reorganize for the new day was undertaken with great enthusiasm.

Even those who move to the suburbs of the suburbs find that the city not only follows them with its perplexing human problems, but that the great majority must daily revisit the city for the work which is their livelihood. Millions hasten back, by train, ferry, and motor car each week-day morning as though they were afraid the city might have vanished the night before.

And the preacher? He must help us redeem the city and use it to the enhancement of the children of God, and for the glory of God, or it will destroy us. But this is not without cost to the preacher. It finally cost Jesus his life. So high a price may not be demanded of us, but we who preach under the judgment of God must pay something—and the final price, if necessary—for the high privilege of sharing in the work of redemption. All Christians who give their pledge of allegiance must pay something, too, no matter where they are or how mobile they may be. The love of God is worth more than money; worth more than a Gothic cathedral of stone; worth more, even, than great fame . . . much more. It is worth a cross.

Only the love of God will cause a preacher to stand firm in the midst of the changing city, and only the love of God can sustain him, as it did Jonah when the wrath of God's judgment finally constrained him to face the problems of Nineveh from whence he had fled. But a more consistent preacher than Jonah is needed. Jonah had more pity on the gourd vine than on the people. And there are too many modern clergymen who evidence a larger interest in what David Barry, Executive Director of Research for the National Council of Churches, calls the "tangible structures of stone that are supposed to be islands of spiritual strength, bastions of defense against a secularized society in which the Church seems irrelevant to most of the decisions that are made," than interest in men—men whom God loved so compassionately that He sent His son to redeem them. God has need to remind us, as He did Jonah, "And should not I spare Nineveh, that great city, wherein there are more than sixscore thousand persons that cannot discern between their right hand and their left hand?" God's interest is *persons*.

Preaching and administering the church to the needs of men in the cities demands a reorganization of techniques. Preaching methods today may have to be considered as much out of order as were John Wesley's methods when he returned to England from his first visit to America. Dr. Harry Emerson Fosdick records in his book, *Great Voices of the Reformation*, that when the pulpits of the Church of England were closed to John Wesley and George Whitfield, they went after the plain people. In one place Dr. Fosdick records the dramatic occasion when Wesley used a chair for a pulpit and a hostile mob for a congregation. Recalling that experience, Wesley wrote:

> The winds were hushed and all was calm and still; my heart was filled with love, my eyes with tears, and my mouth with arguments. They [the mob] were amazed. They were ashamed. They devoured every word.

The city demands men of love who will not let formulas, traditions, institutions, or anything else, trap them into an intolerable position in which the hungry sheep are not fed. It also demands men of great courage who will tackle the enemies of God and man where they are most deeply entrenched.

It is the preacher's responsibility to make a congregation, and as many others as he can, aware of our failure to include our communities in the all-embracing love and concern of Christ. He

must also make us know our need for adaptability instead of for
rigid conventionalism in organization, work, and worship. He
should call the people to daring experiments. Dr. Henry Sloane
Coffin once told the students at Edinburgh, "Surely one new venture a year is not too much to ask a congregation to be willing to
try."

A minister has no alternative but to minister to all the people
within reach of his labors. He must confront his congregation, his
officers, and the larger organizations of his denomination, with
the needs of those outside the church but within reach of the
church. Boldness will be needed in adopting new techniques and
strategies to meet the challenge of the city. As we seek to discover our own individual methods of success, we must work toward greater cooperation and cohesion, because the problems
and the neighborhoods of the city are always inextricably interwoven.

A passage from David Barry's lecture delivered to a conference
of urban pastors is very much to the point:

> What I am suggesting is that the Protestant church in
> American cities is characterized by a series of commit-
> ments to a series of sites that are largely historical
> accidents, meaningful in terms of the residence of Prot-
> estant groups 25 or 50 or 100 years ago, but often quite
> meaningless in terms of service to those groups today.
> We ought to go through our cities, church by church,
> and review those commitments. The purpose of such a
> review should be, not to abandon our older commitments,
> but to give them meaning in terms of specific commun-
> ities. Some church buildings, of course, we should give
> up, but if we do, it should be because a ministry is not
> needed in that particular community, or because another
> kind of building is more suited to our purpose. But for
> the most part, our effort should be to relate our ministries
> to the needs of the people in a particular neighborhood.
> We should use our assets by discovering the specific and
> specialized functions to which they are suited. We should

explore the functions of a church building as a base of
operations rather than as a center of operations.[3]

We may fervently hope and pray that young men looking forward to service in the ministry of the city will take Mr. Barry
more seriously than preachers of an older generation took Dr.
Coffin when he advised them, thirty years ago in his book, *What
To Preach*:

> We must be ready to give up our own preferred ways
> of preaching and conducting public worship if we find
> that we do not reach those without our ecclesiastical
> background. . . . Congregations must be induced to take
> on additional services, or materially to alter one of those
> already in existence, and in many instances be induced
> to increase their contributions to provide for more fa-
> cilities and more workers in order that the church may
> serve the whole neighborhood. And behind whatever
> means are used must be a clear and cogent preaching of
> this ideal of a comprehensive church which embodies
> to the community a social solidarity in Christ.[4]

Because all churches and all people are not ready for new
methods and new strategies is no more reason for holding off
forthright action than it was for St. Paul when he found the people
to whom he preached not ready to receive the gospel. The history
of the early Church records the fact that though many were not
ready for the gospel and many more vehemently opposed it, nevertheless the gospel was irresistible. The vast majority will respond
to firm, responsible, decisive, skillful, and loving leadership. "A
vocal minority, who stand against the dictates of Christian faith,
is by no means unbeatable."

I was once interviewed on a Press Club television program in
Tucson, Arizona. One of the interrogators on the panel told me
with great enthusiasm and approval that he had just learned that
day that the rector of a very exclusive Episcopal parish in which
he grew up back in Chicago had begun street corner preaching.
And he added, "It's about time that all of us began making the

gospel relevant to the problems of our cities and the people about us. If only more ministers had the courage to preach on a corner, as well as in a pulpit, the church would go places." When I reminded him that the rector would need lay support, he replied, "I think I'd be equal to the task."

However, I cannot help but admonish preachers, young or old, that they must not court a peculiar, abstruse, or erratic complex, or even martyrdom. When one does that, he loses effectiveness and power. It is not necessary to put on a hair shirt to please God and discipline the body. Nor is it necessary to join protest movements to cleanse society. Self-discipline is a control of the spirit from within, not an irritation from without. The prophets knew there were no substitutes for a persuasive faith, an unswerving conviction, and methods motivated by compassionate love. If martyrdom is for you, never fear—it will find you out, and by losing your pulpit or even your life, you will become part of the divine process of redemption. But you cannot choose this deliberately, for only God may set this path before you.

The Church may attempt bold methods and even do the unusual, but it must always be a rock of solid substance to which men can anchor their faith, and upon which God can help us build. A minister must always show himself to be such a Christian leader and such a statesman of depth, vision, and understanding that men will turn to him for guidance, even when they disagree with him. The minister who takes a strong position on social, racial, or political questions should always take care to bear the full share of his responsibility to the local parish and the larger church organization. He should also make it a solemn obligation to keep his personal contact as warm and close as possible with those who disagree with him. He should never allow himself to be so isolated that he will be cut off from alternatives. In other words, he should never leave himself in the position where his efforts can be destroyed by attack on the fringes. When the opposition, or those who advance slowly, have no valid arguments against a strong or a right position, they grope for handles. It is relatively easy to destroy, and much more difficult to build or rebuild. Our great task is the laying of solid foundations upon which a genuine, new community of relationship and effort can be built. A wrecking crew needs only strength, anxiety, and vigor; but builders need commitment, sensitivity, imagination, creativity, and patience.

To stop the moral retreat of those responsible for the religious problems of the city, to save the thousands of souls in the "moral jungles of the slums," to redeem the wanderers who go to the ward politician, the proprietor of the corner Bar and Grill, the religious charlatan, the gospel gouger, or the unscrupulous faith healer—to make the gospel relevant to social, labor, and industrial problems, and to redeem the more substantial churches in the more fortunate sections of the cities and the suburbs from apathy, demands something of what Dr. Truman Douglass of the Congregational Board of Home Missions calls "the fresh evangelistic ideals of the East Harlem Protestant Parish."

This group ministry to inner-city church problems was initiated by a group of seminary students at Union Theological Seminary under the leadership of Don Benedict, and has now spread to Cleveland, Boston, New Haven, and Chicago. The young pastors who have dedicated themselves to the task represent Presbyterians, Congregationalists, Baptists, Dutch Reformed, Mennonites, Methodists, Evangelical Reformed, and United Brethren. They have taken over store-fronts, forsaken and dilapidated church buildings in the worst slum areas, in order that they may live in the midst of the situations and conditions of the people to whom they minister. The group ministry they have evolved attempts to develop a shared community life of clergymen and their wives in which they pool all their salaries. Theirs is the roadway presentation of the gospel. They create forms of worship which are consonant with the social and educational level of their parishioners, and they encourage people to share in the creation of these forms.

They have not only been willing to experiment with new forms of worship, new techniques of reaching the unchurched, and new methods of combatting the evils of the community which threaten to destroy the body and the soul—they have done more.

They have disciplined themselves and their families to live the witness that they preach at the very heart of the place where they work. They identify themselves with its misery, hunger, and its physical limitations. Moreover, they do not consider their task as a job vocation from which to gain experience for a larger church or a better paying position, but rather as a mission to which they are ready to devote themselves indefinitely. They say, and rightly so, "a man who elects to answer the call of God's service must distinguish between service and career."

Dean George W. Webber of Union Seminary, a strong supporter of the East Harlem approach, said once:

> If the Gospel can't be made relevant in an industrial and depressed area, it can't have meaning anywhere. . . . We've spent too much time and money on mere church structures, when it isn't the structures that count, but the mass of people . . . We've got to overcome the over-individualism of Protestant sects that has denied a corporate life under Christ. . . . We've got to move in on the de-personalized existence of the slums, whose people are lonely, crass, and materialistic because the whole society around them treats them only as things, not men, and bring these people back to life again.[5]

The East Harlem way, of course, is not the only way to meet the urgent demands of crucial city religious problems, although it is far in advance of the church generally. It is, however, an important pilot for the rest of us. If we would bestir ourselves, we would find many other pilots as well, and greatly extend our present city mission and church extension programs in realistic and vital ways. While we admire the farsighted vision of the East Harlem ministers, and their sacrificial commitment shames us, this is nevertheless a job for the *whole* church. It is infinitely better to tackle the job within the church than to attempt fringe efforts outside the general organization of the church, for lesser efforts always lack permanency.

When efforts are not integrated into the life of the whole church, they are likely to go off at tangents and may become mere sects unless firmly anchored to the on-going life of the church. There are already too many sects encumbering the ground and sapping the strength of the church. We do not need any more. We need the discipline of the denomination, and the denomination needs the challenge and vision which new effort supplies. Furthermore, unless we can develop an overall, total urban strategy, we will continue to dissipate our efforts and our money in experimentation and never come to grips with the roots of the problem.

This is a job for the seminaries, also, for the task begins back in the seminary when the minister is trained for the task. It is an unhappy commentary on religious training that so many preachers find themselves trapped by their own education, unable to relate themselves psychologically and practically to the crucial needs of the hour, or to the grave problems of the city. It is encouraging, however, to note that some of our seminaries are beginning to include courses and seminars designed to relate their students to urban problems. Churches and ministers must rise to the challenge in terms of their capacities and abilities.

One such example—and a good beginning—is that of the women of the Brick Presbyterian church on Park Avenue who formed a Harlem Committee—not to work "for" Harlem, but to work *with* a group of Harlem church women in a mutually co-operative effort which brought both groups into each other's churches.

Another is the Advent Lutheran church which was organized specifically to minister to the blighted area on Milwaukee's south side. Advent was organized to remain and adapt itself to whatever changes of race, national groups, and neighborhood conditions occur. And it has succeeded. Beginning with a hundred seventy-five churchless people, most of whom did not know each other, it grew in a year to over three hundred.

In a similar manner, the suburban church, which has an undeniable right to exist, must relate itself in vital ways to the area which its people have left behind—not merely by gifts of money but through associations of laymen. The focus of responsibility must always be *persons* in areas of opportunity and need. It is not a case of the strong bearing the infirmities of the weak, but of sharing the strength of the strong with the weak for the building of God's Kingdom.

John Wesley, to his eternal credit, was no schismatic. It was no fault of his that the Methodist Church became separated from the Anglicans. To his dying day, he remained a high churchman, even though most of the Anglican pulpits were closed to him. He fought constantly to have his followers become an Order within the Anglican Church. He knew the strength of oneness, which comes from "cross-fertilization"—to borrow a phrase from biology. Just so must we today meet the challenges of religion in the city. The answers must originate from within and remain a part of the whole church.

The problems with which the city confronts the church demand a collegiate ministry. One minister seldom, if ever, has the time, the strength, or the skills to meet the demands placed upon the city ministry. Pastors, religious educators, counselors, social workers, and more and more psychiatrists are needed on our church staffs. The old-time concept of the preacher and his assistants is not good enough for the needs of our cities. The day of the assistant minister as a religious office-boy, subject to the whims of the pastor, is happily over. Only a collegiate ministry elected by the congregation, given equal status and assigned definite responsibilities to meet particular needs, will suffice. The ministry of the Riverside church is a good example of the type of ministry which urban civic and religious problems demand. I might also suggest the type of ministry at the Church of the Master, where I serve as senior pastor with two co-pastors who are equal in all respects. And the three of us are assisted by educators, social workers, and psychologists who share with us the task of making God's love and righteousness relevant to His city children.

The admonition of "the strong bearing the infirmities of the weak" is not limited to money, as people of our time are wont to think. In our finance-conscious society, where money is given an undue emphasis and where even the nation has sought to gear much of its foreign policy to the false conception that economic programs can be supremely effective in a cold war, we need to remind ourselves that all our money is not worth one human soul in the sight of God.

Money is not strength. Our real and only strength is the fellowship of God's love through Christ as we practice it, one for another. Dr. Frank T. Wilson, Dean of the Seminary at Howard University, has wisely and reverently said:

> To experience the love of God in communion with one's fellow human beings is an all-pervading, all-possessing, all-directing encounter. No aspect of life is exempt, no department of existence is immune, no area of behavior is reserved. The Church is uniquely the place where God meets his people and shares with them the heights and depth of His truth, goodness and love. Here, by the working of the Holy Spirit, He leads persons of all ages and conditions into an understanding of their identification, one with another, in all matters pertaining to life and death in this world, and the world to come.[6]

If the Church is to reach the urgent needs of the urban area, its responsible lay and professional leaders need prayerfully to consider their problem in the light of God's love for men, not of men's love for buildings and church appointments. They will have to think of God's desires, not man's wants. They will have to engage in serious study of the urban church problem with scientific detachment. We have not arrived at the place yet where we can see people of all race, age, or station in the universal light of children of God. There is no alternative but for the church to work religiously toward this position, even if white non-Christian, and non-religious persons are at present more welcome in our neighborhood and at our church functions than the most devout Negro, Puerto Rican, or Mexican Christian.

The Christian message is the same, but the witness which motivates and guides the strategy will be different in detail within each city, although similar in overall procedure. Cities, like people, have personalities and differences. Indeed, cities often contain a series of smaller cities within themselves. The present differences have to be met on the merits of the particular situation and the particular implications for the people who live in each area.

We are not helpless, and the situation, though grave, is not hopeless. We have the tools, the resources, the means, and the personnel. Personnel could be unlimited, if we would organize, discipline, and use it. We are short on awareness—but that is slowly coming into focus and supply. We lack strategy, but that can be obtained. All we need is the will to work at the task, not weep over the problems, and the faith to share with God in the extension of His Kingdom for the salvation of men. And this includes a willingness to subordinate all things material—even church buildings.

IV

CRUMBLING FOUNDATIONS

SELDOM in the history of the world have men been as disturbed as they are today by what they hear, feel, and fear; for the foundations upon which we proudly built Western civilization are crumbling.

The immediate past is disturbing, the present uncertain, and the future is dark with a darkness so deep that our wisest statesmen, educators, scientists, and philosophers cannot penetrate it and give us an encouraging word of hope. When they speak, they contradict each other. Their only ground for agreement is uncertainty.

At a time when we have achieved our greatest progress, we seem helpless to find the means to save it. We have been drawn closer to each other by modern means of communication and transportation which have broken down the walls of distance, but we are farther apart in spiritual matters. Spiritual progress has not kept pace with material progress. As space and time have diminished, the ideological and political estrangements have widened, religious suspicions and antagonisms have hardened, and our moral sense has been put into positions of grave compromise.

In its first official estimate of the peril of the "fallout" of radioactive materials of a hydrogen bomb explosion, the Atomic Energy Commission reported that an area the size of New Jersey would be polluted with lethal destruction so terrible that, the Commission added, it hoped "mankind would never experience atomic war." This was a report on only one bomb dropped in the Bikini testing area . . . an experimental bomb, not considered nearly "up to its potential." Science advances today with the speed of a jet plane, and presumably the new tests which have since taken place have indicated a bomb of vast superiority in destructive power. Sir Winston Churchill, in introducing the 1955 defense budget of England, pointed to a dispatch box on the reading desk and said, "It is now a fact that a quantity of plutonium, probably less than would fill this box on the table, would produce sufficient weapons to give undisputed world dominance to any great power which was the only one to have it. There is absolutely no defense against the hydrogen bomb."

One of our foundations—Science—which we trusted to usher in an era of peace, security and safety, has not only crumbled but has left a potentially disastrous situation in its wake of disintegration.

The prospects of the future are alarming, not alone because of the fact that men now have in their hands the power to destroy the world more rapidly than they can rebuild it, but because men hesitate to meet the challenge of moral responsibility and continue to gamble their hopes for survival on the tenuous grounds of their own ingenuity and ability.

Churchill voiced the belief (and there are many who joined and echo him) that the danger of totally destructive war will diminish as all nations reach parity in atomic hydrogen weapons. It is his assumption that realization of the terrible character of the weapon's possibilities for total annihilation will be a deterrent sufficient to ward off the evil day. His classic statement is worth repeating: "By that time, the deterrent may well reach its acme and reap its final reward, enabling tormented generations to march forth serene and triumphant from the hideous epoch in which we have to dwell. Then it may be that we shall by a process of sublime irony have reached a stage in the story where safety will be the sturdy child of terror, and survival the twin brother of annihilation."

Thus up to the present time, the West has put great faith in material technology upon which to build a finer, more productive society. World leaders seem to feel in the final analysis that a positive future can only be anchored to purely negative assumptions: that terrible weapons in the hands of sinful men will create a fear so great that we can only win our race with catastrophe by giving more earnest consideration to means than to ends. But whether we know it or not, there is no longer any hiding place down here. We live in a time which has been more or less accurately described by Jeremiah and Isaiah. Both prophets spoke of the crumbling foundations: "the land shall be desolate, the sown land lies a desert, men taking refuge within woods and caves, the land is all in flight, every city shall be abandoned, under the weight of its transgressions the earth falls down." Dr. Paul Tillich rightly says, "This 'prophecy' is no longer vision, it has become physics."[1]

The signs of decay are so plainly visible in the events of every day and on every side that even those to whom the Bible refers as fools cannot fail to recognize that the decay is farther advanced than we are willing to admit. The restless turning of a radar antenna above the gaudy, broad red-and-white striped huts at the far end of an airport runway, looking with penetrating eyes in all directions in search of an enemy who may come as the terror by night or the arrow that flieth by day, is a clear indication that we have no sure anchorage for our hope. Our civilization has reached a stage where we can no longer be cynical about it.

Neither our cultural attainment nor our advanced knowledge of the science of all aspects of human life, nor our vast resources of wealth, nor our ingenious devices, nor our instruments of war, provide us with peace, security, and hope for a confident future. Hundreds of convenient examples and illustrations are close at hand. Any random sampling leaves a thoughtful person so greatly shaken that he is forced to examine the suppositions upon which our civilization is grounded. He realizes that our Western civilization does not provide the security it once did and in which, until so recently, we wholly relied.

The collapse which is upon us is not of immediate origin. It has been coming for a long time. A number of prophets in Europe and America long ago ran up warning signals which we ignored. Perhaps the blind faith in our remarkable material success and our pride in human ability and achievement made us spiritually too insensitive to read the signs correctly. We confused the symptom of crisis with the cause of crisis, and were content to treat the symptoms and ignore the deep and malignant cause.

Among these prophets were Arnold Toynbee, Albert Schweitzer, Oswald Spengler, Henry Adams, Reinhold Niebuhr, Nikolai Berdyaev, Walter Horton, and many others. But modern prophets can command no more honor, respect, and attention in our times than the ancient prophets did in their day. The despair of the true prophet is as great today as it was in Jeremiah's day when he lamented, "The prophets prophesy falsely and my people love to have it so."

There have always been three kinds of prophets: the true prophet, the false prophet, and the evil prophet. We know much about the first two, but we have thought very little about the last one. We seem to have overlooked him, despite the fact that the world has suffered greatly from him.

The true prophet is respected because of his utter sincerity and his love of his fellow being, but he has few followers—barely a handful of clear-eyed disciples. He is tolerated but almost never loved, because he makes us uncomfortable when he destroys our illusions and pretensions. Sooner or later he is hated, scorned, and persecuted. He finds no joy in saying what he does, and he speaks the judgment of God only because he has no alternative. But because he stands for the truth, history will, in time, validate his message, and then he will be venerated. By then he will be too dead to enjoy it.

The false prophet reaps a lucrative harvest and temporal fame in his lifetime by catering to the whims and egoisms of those sensitized by the true prophet's warnings. He dulls the edge of conscience with the drugs of unfounded optimism. His soothing platitudes make it easy for his followers to disregard their complicity in the evil about to fall upon them, because he tells them what they like to hear and not what they need to know. The false prophet is ignorant of the truth and the love of God. He has no interest in redemption because the present is his all-consuming interest. There are always many more false prophets than true prophets. Their proportion today is about what it was in Elijah's day—four hundred to one.

The evil prophet discerns the truth and actually seeks to escape calamity, but insists upon perverting the truth to support his own sordid purposes. He warns us of our dilemmas, complacencies and confusions, but cunningly attempts—and often with success—to influence us with the designs he has planned for life and history: designs which are created in his own evil image. He understands the depths of our predicament, but he overestimates his ability to bring permanent order out of chaos, and he underrates the extent of God's power. Nor does he know the path of ultimate recovery and salvation. The consequences of the evil prophet's work is a deepening of the tragedy.

Some of the prophets who saw the impending crumbling of Western foundations are not admirable, although we cannot exactly classify them as false prophets. I refer to men like Hitler who long before World War II pointed out in his book, *Mein Kampf*, that the symptoms of decay were, in the last analysis, only consequences of a deeper philosophical breakdown in the racial, economic and cultural world. Other dictators, like Stalin, lost no opportunity to make capital of the collapse. They have tried hard to push it over the precipice of its logical conclusion, and have attempted to usurp the role of God and arrogate power unto themselves. They, and the host of their followers, ride the crest of the flood released by the Christian heresy.

In a large measure, these evil prophets were really revolting against a society which inspired men with great promise of material rewards, but left the soul empty and the world confused and chaotic. Marx and Engels were not false prophets; they were evil prophets. Nevertheless, they gave us clear warning about the collapse of our foundations. Their errors were cut from certain fallacies: oversimplification of the remedies necessary to hold off collapse, a false interpretation of history, overconfident trust in man and the implements he has created, the justification of the most heinous of means to achieve the most doubtful of ends, and finally, the underevaluation and the mislocation of sin in their dogmas, and their attempt to usurp the place and power of God.

Elton Trueblood wrote some prophetic and provocative words back in 1944, almost a year before the crushing defeat of Germany and several years before the rise of the Soviets as a world menace:

> The most dangerous time that Western civilization has known for many generations is immediately before us. It is the period of coalescence. The threat of world tyranny having been surmounted, there will be a strong temptation to suppose that all is well, but the dangers will actually be far greater than they have already been. All kinds of malignant germs will be offered a splendid opportunity for growth in the postwar world.
>
> The sober truth is that as a people we do not believe that we are engaged in a race with catastrophe. We are not aware of the dangers we face, and consequently, we are doing relatively little to meet them. If we could put the same keen intelligence and careful judgment into the revival of faith and the discovery of the proper objects of faith that we put into the production of magnificent machines, man's life on this earth might come into a new and glorious day. We fail to do this because we do not read the signs of the times or listen to the prophets. . . . The West has turned against its own

genius. We have seen it break down before our eyes in the huge and terrifying object lesson of Central Europe. What frightens all reasonable people is the fact that we see about us, in our own neighborhoods, some of the same factors which, existing in greater degree, made the object lesson actual. We are superficially safe in Western democracies so long as war lasts, but the danger will be enormous when the fighting ends. A host of new problems will arise, bringing new temptations.[2]

What Elton Trueblood said in 1944 is also "no longer prophecy." It is reality—and the foremost of this host of new realities is the imperialistic, missionary Communism of the Soviet Union, seeking to entangle the world in its tentacles, and to remake it in its own evil image. Archibald MacLeish, former Undersecretary of State, has accurately described Communism as "the hypocritical protestation of the worst of slaveries . . . the dishonest justification of the most fraudulent of means by the most contemptible of ends." No one, so far as I know, has as yet adequately described our sincere but feverish, and often naive, attempts to defeat Communism with material weapons, but this is, in itself, an indication that we distrust our spiritual foundations.

The Soviets adopted Communism in 1917, although it was a Western creation of Karl Marx and Frederick Engels, men who grew up in Germany at the height of its culture, and who did most of their writing in London and Manchester as a protest against Christian civilization's failure to live up to its own principles in economic, social, and political life. The Soviets further demonstrated that the children of darkness are often wiser than the children of light when they used this heresy of the West as a spiritual tool to break our influence in Asia and Africa, and to disturb us from within by radiating the heresy back to the West.

Communism has shaken the foundations of our world with greater tremors than all previous world catastrophes taken together.

Communism's claim is enhanced in Asia and Africa because it promises to rid those areas of extreme inequalities, and, at the same time, to help them stand up against the West. Soviet Russia may eventually help them to throw off the yoke of Western dominance, but by the time Asians and Africans discover that they have traded one evil for another, the new yoke of Communism will be firmly locked on their shoulders and it will be a long time before they can break it.

Asians and Africans have lost faith in the ability of Christianity to unify the world. Consequently, the initiative is being passed to Communism, since it claims to offer mankind the kind of unity which is the only alternative to the self-destruction of the atomic age. When this comception is linked to an interpretation of history, an eschatology, and a view of man, it creates an illusion which appeals to many who are already disillusioned by the failure of Western civilization to live up to its promises. As a result, Communism as a spiritual weapon, no matter how utterly false it is, becomes a weapon upon which the West has grounded its hopes.

The recognition of this grave crisis in our culture is slowly dispelling our illusions, but it does not provide an adequate substitute to take their place. And the fact that people of our time believe that they have no illusions is in itself the greatest of illusions. We continue with feverish schemes and efforts to stave off disaster without facing up frankly to the dilemma of our pathetic faith in the genius of man and the automatic advance of progress—a progress which we assumed would lead to a higher culture, a peaceful world, a just social order, the elimination of hunger, hate and prejudice. As each scheme fails, we treat its symptoms and we adopt palliatives without reaching back to the underlying source to treat the basic causes. We are no longer optimistic about automatic progress and the goodness of man, but we are no nearer to reliance upon God, nor are we ready to assume responsibility for our share of the trouble in which the world finds itself.

Of one fact, however, there can be no doubt: men are disturbed about the present and discouraged about the future as they have never been before.

We know that something has gone wrong, for the evidence of

it is world-wide. What happens to the West is reflected significantly throughout the world, for the West has penetrated the culture of the world with its religion, its technology, and its economics. Arnold Toynbee, in his excellent little book, *The World and The West*, holds that it is the world and not the West that has had the significant experience of our time. We have assumed that Western impact upon the world was our God-given responsibility, and in a sense it was; but what we have often overlooked is the fact that not all of this impact upon the world has been good, nor has it always been desired by the other peoples of the world.

Africans and Asians, as they rise to think, speak, and act for themselves, indict us as colonizers who prostituted our religion to exploit both the material and human resources of their lands to our own ends. Our recent suffering at the hands of those who suffered for centuries at our hands is a grievous shock to us. We did not conceive that such a thing would be possible in this century. Mr. Nehru is a problem to us, not only because he insists upon opposing Communism in a way that does not seem sound to the West, but because the West is not yet used to Asians talking back, or to their determination to chart their own course of action, irrespective of the West.

But the West, which talked so glibly of the white man's burden, and was to a large extent responsible for world progress and enlightenment (and Asians and Africans would be the first to admit this, with some qualifications), has discovered that its foundations are not as solid as it so readily assumed. It is barely possible that much of the difficulty of our relationship with Red China is cast from a mold older than Communism. Retribution is an inescapable fact, and, as someone has said, history has a long memory.

The rise of nationalism in China would probably, in the long run, have made a non-Red China as intransigent as Communism has. Western actions, attitudes, and relationships to China in the past undoubtedly prepared the fertile political soil in which Communism planted its ideologies, and from which it reaps today's abundant harvest.

Africans and Asians not only rise to indict the West for four and a half centuries of exploitation, but are now making their own decisions about their roles in the world's future. The conference at Bandong in 1955 may well turn out to have been the most important conference of the twentieth century. And perhaps the most significant thing about it was the fact that no Western nations were invited, although many areas under discussion were dominated by Western countries.

Since our foundations are not steady enough for Asians and Africans to build upon, they have determined to build some of their own. Theirs may not be any better than ours, but at this point neither we nor they know that for a certainty. This is a shock to the West, because we have, heretofore, done the thinking for Africa and Asia; we have thoroughly rationalized our domination of the world, and completely justified our exploitation of its resources.

It has been difficult for the West to believe that our foundations could disintegrate so rapidly and so thoroughly. We saw all this coming twenty-five years ago in Asia, but we closed our eyes to the truth. Today we see it developing in Africa as well—and still, our Asian experience has not taught us how to meet the fearful facts. There is as yet no evidence that the West will be any wiser in Africa than it was in Asia.

Because the West has a perverted perspective of its culture, it has been spiritually unprepared to face the real reason for the crisis. It has fought wars, although with such a loathing that measures have been taken to avoid future wars. Conferences, treaties, leagues, systems of collective security, economic and social measures, have been piled one upon another to shore up our sinking foundations. Yet they have been of little use. The last war drew to its close in 1945 and we still have unresolved, intermittent, localized, but terribly expensive hot and cold wars which reach no real or permanent settlement. We continue to make temporary settlements, accept issues with a sense of tragic fatality, or pin our hopes to the machinery of political arrangements. We continue to prepare for defense, and attempt to control the forces of history by intellectual formulas created by men.

The trouble is not with the formulas, but with the fundamental premise of *laissez-faire*. Charles Kean wrote in *Christianity and the Cultural Crisis:*

> In a society which views intellectual processes as primarily a search for external facts in order to control them, the intellectual problem posed by war results in frustration. In a society which views political activity as a service in behalf of economic enterprise, whether private or commercial, the political problem posed by war is insoluble. In a society which regards morality as a code that men adjust in order to avoid trouble, the moral problem posed by war leads to despair.[3]

The despair is written in letters so large that people who travel as rapidly as we do today can read the words even without slowing down.

When we found that our civilization lacked the security we had attributed to it, our romantic idealism gave way to disillusionment, and disillusionment to skepticism. Grave questions were raised about the worth of human civilization, the omnipotence of God, the value of culture, the possibility of world peace, the goodness of man, and the necessity of religion. Men readily understood that moral failure to match our scientific achievement with religious insight left a spiritual vacuum, but they were incapable of placing themselves and their technology under the judgment of Christian morals and ethics. The learning and knowledge by which the world advanced so fast and so far thus failed us at the very moment when they came into full and complex maturity. With the flowering of human genius, man realized that he had not developed inner resources—the wisdom and the will to bring about the good life of which his inventions were the symbols. Secularism, implicit and explicit, ruled the day.

Despite the fact that the rational arguments for belief in the theistic foundations of religion remain unshaken, the signs of the decay of our Christian faith and action are all about us. We still call our civilization Christian, but this may be no more than a frame of reference to which we are accustomed because of its accomplishments in the past. We present impressive figures on the growth of church membership, but there is no corresponding evidence of its impact on the morality of our society.

The figures for New York City for 1954 showed that Catholics made up forty-seven per cent of the population, Jews twenty-six per cent, and Protestants, twenty-two per cent: a total of ninety-five per cent. The figures are impressive, but when we notice the increase of crime and corruption, the political abuse and graft, the moral decay of our youth, the breakdown of the home, the attitude toward gambling—it becomes "legal" for the purpose of supporting religious institutions—the figures do not present a convincing argument for the religious penetration of our lives or our social order. Religion is often reduced to a fetish to be trotted out in a crisis. People join churches, but few of them read the Bible or basically change their lives. Our religious institutions are broad and expansive, but the dimensions of faith seldom penetrate beneath the surface or indicate any depth of insight or height of living which would substantiate the protestations of our faith.

There are many evidences of the failure of our secular society. The marriage vow is taken less and less seriously. Men and women increasingly contemplate this contract, not as a sacramental act, but as a convenience to be tried as an experiment and rejected without difficulty or regret if it fails to satisfy. We often exhibit a higher regard for the means than the ends. Mission executives appear to have greater faith in their organization than in the faith which the organization was created to spread, with the result that the missionary enterprise is often trapped by its machinery at the very moment when it should be most creative and spontaneous in winning souls to the kingdom. Political corruption in a Christian democracy is condoned, or at best, ignored as a necessary evil which must coexist with the democratic process.

Standards of conduct are shaped to our caprices. Newspapers across the land pump for relaxation of gambling laws in order to accommodate the lowest instincts of men, or to secure increased state and city funds for hospitals and welfare institutions. Power

politics—the effort to organize human life apart from moral inhibitions, and the desire to influence international decisions by
the weight of money and military strength—have become the
basis for international diplomacy. There is an increased reliance
upon a strong central authority because individual helplessness
is felt so strongly in an age which began with revolt against authority. The professed belief in the equality of men is coupled
with such complex reservations that many of us are left in an immoral hegemony where all others are equal—after us. The willingness to let the government assume more and more responsibility for the organization of our lives, individually and collectively, has reached the point where we consider paternalism the
natural order of things. Finally, the breakdown of the influence
of the home is cracking the very basis of a sound society.

The end is bound to be moral chaos. The external, material
structure of civilization will stand for a while, and a certain measure of progress and advance will continue, but skepticism will
degenerate into cynicism, and cynicism will breed inner contra-
dictions.

> Any culture disintegrates when its inner core of religious
> conviction gets too much out of harmony with its outer
> shell of material culture and technique . . . Advanced
> civilizations lose their heart when religion becomes a
> department of life, coordinate with politics, economics,
> and fine arts, instead of being the center and source from
> which they must continually return for judgment and
> redirection.[4]

Life then becomes empty. But life never remains empty, for
nature abhors a vacuum both in the realm of the physical and of
the spiritual. Just because powerful forces must rush in to fill it
up, a vacuum is dangerous. In Germany, emptiness was filled
by the false religion of National Socialism; in Italy by Fascism;
and in Russia by Communism. Today Communism attempts to fill
the spiritual vacuum of every place on the globe.

At the same time that a breakdown manifests itself from within,
the recrudescence of Eastern religions is challenging the Christian

foundation of our relationship with the East. Buddhism, Islam, and Hinduism are the chief threats to the ascendance of Christianity. Moslems are beginning a crusade in Africa, south of the Sahara, which has already met with considerable success. When Colonel Nasser, the Prime Minister of Egypt, returned from his pilgrimage to Mecca in August, 1954, he called upon the Moslem world to raise a missionary fund of fifty million dollars to carry on proselytization of Africans. I personally talked with Moslems from the Middle East and Pakistan who were already at work along the West Coast of Africa. They are financed by Saudi Arabia oil profits and the Moslem Brotherhood.

This is no idle threat. Moslem nations no longer allow Christian missionaries free movement within their lands. In Pakistan, a Christian may enter only as a teacher, not as a preacher. The Indian government, which maintains a secular veneer over a revitalized Hinduism, put stringent limitations on Christian missionaries in 1953. When I was in India in 1951, I chanced upon a statement issued by a group of enlightened Hindus which promised to evolve a better role for individuals and a higher way of life than Christianity. I spoke with a few Indian Christians who were so critical of Western Christianity's failure to live up to its creed that they considered it their Godly duty to *oppose* vigorously any further extension of our missionary effort.

Islam demonstrated, once before, its missionary ability to challenge Christianity in Asia and Africa. Although it began its work in North Africa three centuries after Christianity, it won twice as many converts as all the forces of Christianity. In the seventh century, it moved across North Africa to Spain; and after the eleventh century it moved eastward through Persia and India to Indonesia and the southern anchor of the Philippine archipelago, the island of Mindanao. Its present success shows that it still has a powerful appeal as a counter-movement of reform.

Buddhism and Confucianism have been more tolerant of Christianity's missionary efforts than has Islam. But even so, their philosophical traditions, although not violently antithetical to Christianity, have been harder to penetrate because the point of confrontation has been so illusive. When I was in Japan, I was in-

vited to speak on social, economic, and political subjects in many
Buddhist temples. In Nagoya, a group of priests told me of the great
Indian convert to Buddhism, King Asoka. Asoka was won to Buddhism in 261 B.C. at the height of his military conquests, which
stretched from the Deccan plateau to the Himalayas. Abandoning
his military ambitions, he devoted his ability and energies to missionary Buddhism. He sent missionaries to Ceylon, Indo-China,
the Middle East, Java, and China, from whence their message
spread to Japan. Buddhism, through Asoka's efforts, changed the
whole of the Far East and left a cultural deposit which still thrives.

Although the Buddhist fear that the Christian missionary's activity is a covering for political acts may not be as evident as the
Hindu or the Moslem fear, it is just as real. This is a point at which
Christian missions have to exercise great care, since in the past
they have been undeniably linked to Western economics and
business, and, even more closely, with colonial penetration.

In China, Western technology bred a disastrous political corruption; in Japan, it led to an equally disastrous militarism which
gave the West its first hint that its position in the Far East was not
impregnable. The outcome in India is still in doubt. What the
future holds in Africa is not yet clear because Africa has no
old and well-developed religion, and the issue has not yet been
completely joined. But that time will come sooner than we think,
surely within the next decade.

A quarter of a century ago, the West was more concerned
about what Great Britain thought in India, the Dutch in Indonesia,
the French in Southeast Asia, and its own consular and business
officials in China, than it was about what was stirring in the minds
of the people in those areas. Today we must deal with indigenous leaders and the masses of Asia. We may still be orientated
to colonial officials in Africa and to the Afrikanders in South Africa
but very shortly we will be obliged to face the problem of orien-
tating to African leaders, to African men and women.

It is still hard for most Westerners to believe that a political
catastrophe has come out of Africa to overtake us. But that is what
we thought only a few years ago about China—a span of time within the memory of most of us. All the while, Communism is con-

stantly at work to exploit colonialism and deepen the hostility of Africans toward Europeans. Its glittering promises are a powerful enticement in the face of increased African disillusionment with Western rulers. The situation cannot be attributed to an act of God nor to senseless laws of nature. We cannot excuse our failures by claiming a loss of command over the environment, nor the greater zeal of alien doctrines like Communism.

Toynbee, in his monumental *A Study of History* attributes the breakdown of our civilization—like all others that have met their doom—to national and cultural suicide. The problem is from within, not from without. Our greatest problem is a spiritual problem. Unless this problem is solved, civilization fails. Man's sinful nature is such that he will use his knowledge for evil unless there is something above and beyond him to turn his knowledge into beneficent ways. He will set the pride of his difference, achievement, culture, and race against every other man, and even against God if he is not warned. And he will, more often than not, delude himself into believing that the survival of his institutions—which he protects long after their usefulness is past—is as important as the survival of his ideals.

There are many in our time who would like to reduce human conduct to neat little equations of causality with which scientific theories can deal—equations which rule out the inexplicable motivations of the human heart and soul, the mysteries of religion, the will of God, and His designs of love for men in a Kingdom of righteousness. And there are also those who believe that brotherhood is an idle speculation—at its best, an impossible ideal, at its worst, a contradiction of man's natural arrogance and antagonisms; that war is inevitable, and lasting peace an impossible dream.

The only possible consequence of such pessimism and skepticism is a collapse of the foundations upon which humanists and secularists have morbidly built. Lacking transcendental guidance, they have no star of hope beyond themselves by which they can evaluate their ideas or their methods. The consequences of their own failures are upon them, and they lack the insight to escape disaster.

V

PREACHING TO
PRESERVE A NATION

IT IS said that a man must set his own house in order before he can tackle the problems of the world. It is true, if only for the lesson in humility it teaches.

Among colonial peoples we see that Western culture has failed because it has not been linked to a true Christianity. But are we as easily shocked when we see, at home, how the religion of Jesus has been reduced to vassalage to economics, science and politics?

Many good people insist that "politics has no place whatever in the church, and the preacher should never mention it from his pulpit." A layman of a large New York church recently spoke these words at a conference, and he continued, "Politics and religion are as different as night and day; they have no relationship to each other at any point. They are as separate as oil and water. Let the politicians have their work, but let the church be the church."

When a minister in the audience mildly disagreed with this, and said: "In that case, then we'd better take all the Old Testament prophets out of the Bible," the elder excoriated him in a voice strident with anger.

But the young clergyman had made a telling point. The prophets of old were always applying the high moral demands of religion to the political systems by which men organized their lives. Yet despite such evidence in the writings of the prophets, an uncomfortably large section of the Christian Church wants no relationship whatever between religion and politics.

Corruption in politics and government has led many of our citizens to the false assumption that religion and religious leaders have no place there. One often hears it said by the "best people" that the dirt of ruthless politics and the cynicism of politicians creates an atmosphere which no religious man should enter if he wishes to maintain his honesty and integrity. Some go so far as to say that "good people" can have little or no influence in the political arena, because, in the end, they will be obliged to compromise with evil and will thus be contaminated by the very evil they originally set out to purge. This is true only so long as some men wish it and others allow it. Is not good more powerful than evil, is not righteousness more powerful than injustice? If our abdication of political responsibility is any barometer, then many Christians are either hopelessly irresponsible or simply do not believe that righteousness *is* a force more powerful and more persuasive than evil.

There is not one prophet in the whole of the Old Testament who did not at one time or another preach to the multitudes about their collective duties, who did not advise kings and governors on matters domestic and foreign, who did not condemn injustice and corruption, both political and moral, who did not inveigh against the attempt of a king or a country to usurp the place of God, who did not encourage honest, sincere, and responsible group action, and who did not exhort individuals to rise to their duty if they would preserve their privileges and save their lives. Yet the prophets were not interested in particular forms of gov-

ernment and systems of politics; what concerned them deeply
was whether a form of government and a system of politics
measured up to the righteous will of God, and whether those
forms and systems served the best interests of individuals and the
unity and preservation of the community. It is the sum total of the
Old Testament, spelled out clearly chapter by chapter, page
on page, age after age.

The twenty-first chapter of the first Book of Kings tells the
story of Ahab's theft of Naboth's vineyard; and the eleventh
chapter of the Second Book of Samuel tells the story of David's
lustful appropriation of Bathsheba, the wife of Uriah—a woman
of beauty whom he seized as a piece of property. The stories
are not so much about Ahab and David as they are about the prophets, Elijah and Nathan, who condemned the kings and brought
them face to face with the judgment of God upon the injustice
of their acts.

Neither Nathan nor Elijah were living and speaking under the
dispensation of the Christian Gospel, which we claim to be the
highest revelation of God. Nevertheless they so strongly believed that both king and commoner are subject to the same moral
law that they risked banishment—and even death—to confront
the great men of their day with that law.

God was and is concerned with the rights, justice, and the
liberties of his children—even the humblest of them. Our Lord
Jesus turned aside from his mission of building the Kingdom to
answer the cry of one solitary person in need. Now as then we
need prophetic voices to protest irresponsible actions. We must
protest the act, for example, of the Commissioner of Licenses in
California, who brushed aside the pleas of a small church, completely ignoring that church's rights and even the zoning laws of
the commonwealth, to grant to a huge grocery chain a license to
operate on Sunday and a second license to sell liquor. Alas, there
was no prophetic voice to speak powerfully for political justice,
and the church lost.

In our day we believe that a nation, as an individual, is not above
the law. How then can a minister of the gospel avoid taking a stand

in the realm of politics? The roots of our political society are grounded in God's will and love; the spirit of our nation is based on the spirit of Christianity. That spirit is being violated day by day. Are we to be silent?

In the fifth chapter of Exodus, one reads the story of Moses pleading for the release of the children of Israel from the involuntary chains of bondage. A similar problem once greatly troubled the American conscience. That was a century ago—but today there are people in political bondage all over the world, even among our "allies." In South Africa, for example, where an element of the Church of England stands up nobly to a ruthless government, we Americans are involved in the slavery and injustice of that sad and frightening land more deeply than we think. We so vehemently protest against injustice, denial of liberty and human rights behind the iron and bamboo curtains—and at the same time we remain silent about abuses perpetrated with equal violence and disaster against the sons of God in South Africa! In the past ten years American capital has been increased fifteen hundred percent in the industries of that nation. (These are the statistics Prime Minister Strijdom quotes whenever he is asked if his policies of disenfranchisement of the African will harm South African relations with the United States.) Our United Nations' delegate never votes against South Africa's refusal to allow the United Nations to enter the Trusteeship Areas it controls. Who is to point up the immorality of our nation's dual role? What institution but the Church, which is the body of Christ, and her ministers, who are the agents of God?

Was it not the prophet Samuel who counseled the people of Israel on the choice of King Saul? (1 SAMUEL 10:24) Is it not within the province of the minister to counsel the people on the choice of the men and women who seek to lead the destiny of our country, to point out their virtues and their shortcomings, and thereby to help insure the selection of honest, decent, able, and sincere public officials? I heard a minister of one of our most famous churches say that he had never publicly or privately supported a candidate for office in his whole life. Yet I, along with others, had to go to his assistance when a city official wrongly interfered with his right to minister to one of his communicants in a hospital.

When Sennacherib was investing the ramparts of Judah, Hezekiah sought the wisdom and the guidance of Isaiah. That story is written in chapters eighteen and nineteen of Second Kings. Isaiah did not withhold his advice any more than we should—although how many mayors, governors, or presidents, not to mention kings and premiers, ever seek the counsel of clergymen on anything but the most trivial matters? We should hardly be surprised that the representatives of the Roman Catholic and Protestant churches, and rabbis of the Jewish community, were refused permission by the Senate Foreign Relations Committee of the United States to attend the original hearings on American plans for international cooperation in the post-war years.

For that matter, who in authority has paid any attention to the Asia missionaries who saw the present events shaping up in the Orient a quarter of a century ago? By like token, is it surprising that no one listens to those former old China hands who are now at work in Africa? Yet in China they read the signs of the times rightly, and in Africa, during the summer of 1954, they told me, without a single exception, that they see the same events shaping up on that continent.

This follows an old and classic failure of men. During the reign of Jeroboam, two thousand years ago, Amos preached against corruption in high places (AMOS 7:10) and pled for justice and decency for the poor and for fair wages and the rights of the laborers. But what he said was not taken seriously until he spoke up in the King's court and in the King's own chapel. Then however, Amaziah, the priest, told the sheepherder from Tekoa, whom God had called to prophesy, that he could not give the word of God's righteousness in the King's court and chapel because it contradicted the will of the King and the advice of his courtiers. It was all right to condemn Edom, Damascus, Gaza, Tyrus, Moab, and all the rest, but not the transgressions of Israel and Judah. That was different. Were they not the Lord's own chosen people?

So today, it is proper to condemn Red China and the Soviets for the debacle in Indo-China, but not France or South Africa or Spain. That is different. They are our friends. Speak softly about the Congo and South Africa. There is uranium there, and we need that. As for ourselves, we must not be criticized—at least not too harshly.

We still have Amaziahs with us to this very day; Amaziahs who completely identify themselves with parties and ideologies and political movements—something no minister should do to the extent that his judgment becomes clouded to God's higher demands.

"Woe to them that decree unrighteous decrees, and that write grievousness which they have prescribed." That is Isaiah talking (ISAIAH 10: 1). He is still considered sound in the church, and of a worthy and righteous reputation, is he not? Yet everyone of us is familiar with a time in our country when a United States Senator castigated anyone who took exception to his decrees about the security of the nation, nor will they soon forget the almost heinous methods he used.

And what should a preacher say when some of the states deliberately flout the Supreme Court by trying to circumvent its rulings by the enactment of evasive legislation? Should he keep silent and hold his peace? Even silence might conceivably be better than the action of the Methodist bishops of the Southeastern Conference meeting in Charlotte in 1955. The bishops said, "We doubt that the healing of the world's woes is sometimes furthered by readjustment of human institutions; and the enactment of laws with an element of compulsion about them may not, therefore, be the most effective."

There are many of us who do not favor the use of law to force people to act in accordance with the Christian ethics which they proclaim, but sometimes—after all other means have been patiently exhausted—society is left with no choice. The bishops went on to say they believed that racial segregation in their section of the country "protected the rights and privileges of minorities." How this squares with the gospel of Jesus in the light of the situation which obtains in the areas of their jurisdiction, the bishops did not tell us. They went on to say that the spiritual force of the church, and not the enactment of laws, was the most effective means of solving the problem of segregation. Ideally speaking, they are right; but they have not put the ideal into practice.

Enactment of law and political stratagems have advanced the cause of racial justice and the protection of individual and group rights far more effectively thus far than has the church. The highest court of California recently overruled a lower court which had previously sustained a city official who refused a marriage license to an interracial couple. Said the chief justice in handing down the decision, "The right of persons in a free society to choose their mates is the highest personal privilege." Yet the clergyman who performed the ceremony, although he had never encouraged interracial marriages (nor was it a Negro-white marriage), lost his pulpit!

Turn to the headlines of the morning newspaper in any city in the nation: they tell the same story day after day. One cannot read the tragedy of our time without immediately recognizing that the voice of the minister is still needed in the same context as the voice of the prophet. It is an old story: there is nothing new about it under the sun. We find account after account of political corruption, theft of public funds, collusion of public officials with gamblers, abuse of the public trust by men in high places, graft in low-cost housing construction, crime protected by guardians of public safety, ticket-fixing for traffic violations, intimidation of citizens and shake-down of merchants, income tax evasion with the connivance of collectors of internal revenue, miscarriage of justice in the courts, denial of the right to vote, unjust and preferential legislation.

So the story runs, as sad today as ever before. It is enough to turn one sour . . . but not enough to make one despair! It is immoral and unethical to demand the privilege of freedom and democracy without accepting its responsibilities and the duties which evolve therefrom. There is absolutely no purpose in talking about injustice or corruption or even privileges in a democratic society unless we exercise our freedom to oppose the injustice and corruption and to enlarge our privileges. We must do more than talk. We must *work* at the political machinery to achieve a good and just society, or we may see it disappear before our eyes.

One of the most encouraging experiences I ever had with government officials was when I was invited to speak to a group of State Department officers in Washington. To my great and enjoyable surprise, I found that a hundred or more of these men gathered for lunch once or twice a month for Bible reading, prayer, and discussion, as they sought the will of God for their task and for our nation. But this does not get into the newspapers. It is not news, and some misguided Christians would even condemn them for "mixing politics with religion."

Is it not the duty of the preacher to apply the high moral demands of Christianity to the ethics of government officials; vigorously to oppose political corruption, malfeasance in office, and cheap politics? And is it not also his obligation to encourage both the laity and the clergy to greater concern with the moral problems of the city, state and nation, and to help bring the impact of religion to bear on the life of the nation? The preacher must preach as creatively, as forthrightly, and as courageously as possible to the corporate life of our people, when and as occasion and situation demand. He should have the purification and transforming of society—in the light of the Lord and for the preservation of the nation—as the aim uppermost in his heart and mind.

If the morning newspaper does not sufficiently draw our attention to the complicity of modern Christians in the political life of the community and the nation, then turn to the final edition of the evening paper and see the same story: how politics and government more and more affect every aspect of our existence. As men live longer and as the population increases, the government takes more and more of our income, and it regulates more and more of our lives. Many clergymen who are now accepting social security benefits never troubled themselves to support that legislation. Labor legislation affects relations between labor and industry, and often determines whether we have transportation, or whether the city has fuel, or babies have milk; it establishes the conditions under which men may earn a living, and protects their rights to bargain collectively. These problems are continually subject to government supervision and review. Various forms of unemployment insurance, proposals for a basic wage, and subsidies to farmers are debated, passed, and revised.

Since most Christians do not tithe, we give the church what we think we can afford, but the government demands a percentage of our income and sets penalties upon every one of us who does not comply. (Most of us do not begrudge income tax, although there are some citizens, and among them some religious leaders and Christian laymen, who work harder over the loopholes in the law which are to their advantage than they do over their conscience.) The list can be added to indefinitely, because hundreds of bills to regulate and affect our lives are introduced in city councils, state legislatures and the Congress, every month they are in session.

The state of California amended its constitution with a law providing for a loyalty oath as a prerequisite for tax-exemption, churches included. Fortunately, the amendment was ruled unconstitutional. But the state attorneys decided to appeal the decision, and some of the legislators began writing a new bill which would achieve the same effect.

There is every reason for ministers to be concerned with the government of our society, for a government controlled by politicians—good or bad—slowly, imperceptibly, but forcefully encroaches upon our independence. We could easily awaken one day to find ourselves totally dependent upon the government. There can be no doubt about these facts: namely, that all of us are losing more and more of our independence; that some of us are losing our self-determination; and not a few are losing our self-respect. The process of this erosion absolutely reverses the principle we hold as sacred: that government in a democracy is derived from the consent of the governed for the needs of the governed. Jesus said, "The sabbath was made for man, and not man for the sabbath." We seem to be moving toward the point where government is not made for man, but man for the government.

It ought to be fairly clear that the kind of world we want and the kind of government we need—one within which men can achieve the kind of lives God wants them to live—does not emerge out of a vacuum. Good, clean, wise, and honest government does not just happen while we stand irresolutely on the side lines. As Lord Bacon once said, "It is reserved only for God and the angels to stand on the side lines." But even God takes a hand. Jesus said, "My father worketh hitherto, and I work."

The selfhood which achieves the dignity which God intended has to be cultivated in an environment of decency, justice, honor, righteousness, and security, based on solid moral and spiritual foundations.

Instead of trying to help keep religion out of politics, as so many clergymen and Christian laymen have naively undertaken to do, we ought to be putting religion squarely at the heart of the political crisis of freedom in government.

Everyone should be able to see that the crisis of freedom is the crisis of faith. Democracy is a system of political organization based on faith: faith of men in God and in one another; faith in the ultimate worth of men as sons of God and as individuals; faith in the moral law; faith in the possibility of redemption and the power of love; faith that in the final analysis right overcomes all obstacles. And, as Elton Trueblood declares:

> Just as some declare their faith in science without inquiring sufficiently into the structure that makes science possible, others assert their faith in democracy without probing too deeply into the grounds of its existence. But a democratic way of life can by no means stand alone. Its success or failure depends not primarily upon political techniques, but on the unargued principles and premises which the citizens of a democracy already use. Ulti-

mately, it depends upon the faith of the people, and this fact is demonstrated by the failure of the most modern democratic techniques when the supporting faith is weak or non-existent. . . . Democracy does not succeed by counting votes; it depends far more on whether we retain the essential dignity of man. Can man, the individual, respect himself and his neighbor? If he cannot, the most elaborate system will break down.[1]

In American society, politics and government are nearly synonymous. In fact, politics *is* government, and we have no less an authority for this statement than former President Harry S. Truman. Dwight D. Eisenhower always hated "politics," but soon after he took office he found that he too had to become involved in politics in order to achieve his aims. Politics is the way we write our laws, elect our officials, create our services, organize our protection, handle our collective problems of welfare, and govern ourselves. We simply cannot have good government without good politics. But good politics depends upon good men. It is the duty of religious institutions and their leaders to prepare such leaders and to inspire and undergird them, and to hold the ultimate goals of God's judgment ever before them. Most Christians hold politicians in contempt, or merely tolerate them. Politicians, however, often influence our government and its legislation far more significantly than all ministers, priests, and rabbis taken together.

Many of our ablest and best laymen refuse to work in politics and shy away from public service because they are afraid of contamination. Many ministers and religious persons have no dealings with politicians because they are afraid of the association and dislike politicians' methods. Many such persons not only refuse to work in politics and government, but despise it altogether. Many others are so pessimistic that they do not even vote in elections. Such lack of positive acceptance of civic responsibility is a denial of Christian hope. We often hear people say, "It won't do any good. The political situation is too complicated and too deeply rooted to be changed. Religion will make no difference."

Nonsense—absolute nonsense! "Else the God in whom we believe is fiction." Not so! He is imminent—moving through history and in society. If a minister cannot preach that the power of God, working through consecrated men and women, can change a political situation—if he cannot proclaim the fact of Christian redemption down through history—then we ought to take "Thy kingdom come and Thy will be done on earth" out of the Lord's Prayer right now. Dr. James Moffatt beautifully translated one phrase in the New Testament, "The Kingdom of God tarries, but we lay hold with impatient hands upon it to bring it in." Christian faith has always anchored its hope in the lives of consecrated individuals—even in one man.

"Religion will make no difference"?—it is still nonsense, even if Mark Hanna did reply to Wayne Wheeler (when the latter told him the Christian folk of his state would support an honest candidate for office), "Young man, your kind of folk are all right in a prayer meeting, but not worth a hoot in a political caucus." Christian folk could make all the difference in the world in a caucus or an election or an international meeting if they would only use the power and privilege at their disposal. That is what William Lloyd Garrison did, even though they dragged him through the streets of Boston. All he had were some fine ideas about freedom and men, a little ink, some paper, and the faith that righteousness ultimately triumphs over evil. A later generation erected a monument to him not far from the place where he had been dragged over the cobblestones.

If we do not believe that "good persons" can go into politics—and God knows they are needed there, either as lay or professional workers—and make a profound impression for good upon it without being corrupted themselves, then we simply do not believe our basic religious protestations that righteousness is more powerful than sin, and that justice triumphs over injustice. The "good people" of our municipal localities need to reaffirm their faith in the ancient religious fact that importunity for the right and for decency wins consent, even against the most reluctant rascals and the most deeply entrenched wrong. Many of our deficiencies in government and politics can be traced to a false neutrality which many Christians, especially some Protestants, have assumed in regard to politics.

We cannot extricate ourselves from some responsibility toward politics and government, even when we take no direct part in them. By our refusal to act in a situation where great issues and principles are at stake, we unconsciously throw our weight on the side which is the stronger contender. Unwittingly, we often help the worst side and the least desirable cause. The Psalmist wrote a long time ago, "We are (inextricably) bound in the hurdle of life."

Criticism of failures, and protests about the corruption which abound on the political horizon, are not the limits of religious participation in politics and government. Mere abstract goodness is not enough. God does not stand apart from even our most sordid situations. God is transcendent but also imminent in every human situation as the supreme Doer of Good. It is therefore to the reformer, the prophet, the leader who labors, and to those who do the good they know to be good, that we give our greatest homage. Jesus said, "Be ye not only hearers of the word, but doers."

Unless we translate our beliefs into practical action on the political level, the things we care for most in our society will be left to the mercy of those for whom we care the least. Citizens in a democratic society, when faced with overwhelming problems, are never justified in refusing to do the good they can, simply because they cannot do all the good they would like to do. This is the main point in Jesus' story of the talents.

Men bought our democratic form of government with their lives. They pledged their fame and their fortunes to secure it. They developed it through hardship with heroic devotion. Some of these men and women lived even before the time of the Renaissance and the Reformation. There was Jesus dying on the cross to tell us that the truth of freedom and the ultimate worth of every individual is at the center of life and the heart of God. "If the truth will set you free, you shall be free indeed."

In one sense, at least, freedom may be said to be the very image of God. This is not freedom from something like tyranny, oppression, or hunger, but freedom to be something more than previously experienced—something akin to the will of God. Those who put the emphasis on the Pilgrim Fathers' flight from tyranny and oppression miss the point almost entirely. They were not so much running away from something as they were running toward something—a pursuit, if you please. A pursuit of the dream of the right to worship God; the desire to put God's righteous will at the center of all human action; the right to have a valid voice in society; the right to protect the right of others to worship God. They were seeking the right to labor in the continuing creative efforts of God for a better world in which better men might more nearly become the sons of God. They were in pursuit of freedom to be and to do; freedom to do the will of God was their purpose in founding this nation. This kind of freedom supersedes all other freedoms, and unites and gives them their ultimate purpose and meaning.

When the concept of freedom is misunderstood, it leads all too easily to license. But even understood freedom is not a valid concept except it be considered in relation to some power which grants it and which thereby places limits upon it. Many Christians in our day think of freedom as the right to ignore the very grounds upon which freedom is possible—the right to ignore the democratic process and decisions which make democracy possible, and the right to be free of involvement in the machinery of politics and government. If this be the freedom we prize, then heaven help us.

But this is not the freedom we prize, for freedom is not a detachment. It is not an unconditioned idea of life without responsibilities, physical and moral. "When we have reached the point of measuring the stature of our freedom by the height of the pile of our discarded inhibitions, is anyone minded to die for this eviscerated ghost. . . ."[2] Men have died, but for something more akin to God than that, and they keep on dying for it in Asia and in Africa, as well as in China. And whether we see and hear the proof of it or not, there are some who die for it in Russia.

The concept of freedom as freedom *from* something is a quixotic thing. Socrates was free to choose death for an ideal which he believed to be the truth, and Jesus was free to sacrifice himself for what he knew to be the truth. Although one cannot be equated with the other, neither was free to escape the obligation of his freedom. St. Paul in his prison cell purchased the right to be there by his indomitable stand on the great questions of his time, but he was free to have done otherwise. There have been a host of others—Huss at his stake, Luther before his emperor, and Knox before his queen.

Democracy based upon freedom is a form of government which attempts an ideal association of men, but it has to be achieved and managed by practical day-by-day means. This is called politics—a much-abused word which suffers chiefly because selfish men abuse it and professional politicians use it, not always so much for the common good as for the ends of a particular party, clique or selfish interest. Every one of us cherishes the freedom we enjoy, but many of us despise the means by which we achieve it.

Democratic participation in the machinery is a necessary obligation, binding upon all who live under it, or who accept any measure of the freedom it provides. To refuse to accept the responsibility of freedom is the surest guarantee that we will lose that priceless heritage. The Communists, the Fascists, and the dictators know this, so their first concern is to limit the rights of the individual and to curb his freedom of thought, action, religion, and association. Democracy is therefore a never-ending pursuit to achieve a more ideal association of men, in which both their freedom and their responsibilities are enlarged.

Religion in its essential nature touches human life and relationships at every point. Religion is never apart from life, but is a part of life, for it deals not merely with the great metaphysical truths of origin, purpose, reason for existence, and the destination of man, but also with what befalls him on the way as he lives and moves in the world. Religion permeates all our social relationships. It sets our goals and ideals and leads us to the discovery and realization of our highest potentialities for a better way, a better self, and a better society, collectively and individually. Its chief aim is to evolve as nearly an ideal society as possible, and to so inspire and discipline men that they can be fit citizens of that society.

It is a shallow and superficial view of religion which limits it to a mere formal expression of individual relationship to the divine Creator for the tenuous goal of personal salvation without any bearing upon the problems which most deeply trouble all our society. Strange but true, the fanatically religious person who wants to exclude the influence of religion and Christians from politics and government arrives at the same conclusion that the corrupt politician and the unfaithful government servant have already adopted for entirely different reasons. The former, unintentionally, by his failure to bear witness to the truth of religion in all life's efforts, unconsciously aids the latter in their evil and perfidious designs. Many politicians would like nothing better than for the clergy to keep silent and hold themselves aloof from politics and from political questions. The waning of religious influence in politics and government always creates a moral vacuum which inevitably brings in its train spiritual impoverishment, cynicism, corruption in society, and decadence.

The religion of Jesus devotes itself to the tasks of providing the righteous wellspring of a purposeful existence, out of which democracy flows. Christians have always believed—although some of us have not acted on our beliefs or carried them out to their logical conclusions—that all government is under the judgment of God and responsible to His righteous Will. The Christian religion, especially the Protestant interpretation of it, has always held that it is a Christian duty to work for the best possible government.

Our religion has never endorsed any form of government, although the democratic form of government we know and enjoy is a product of the Protestant faith and life. Walter Lippman points out that too many politicians try to determine what is right and what is wrong by votes. He goes on to remind us that what is right and what is wrong, "is not mere moonshine and cobwebs," but "a mandate of heaven."[3]

Jesus paid taxes to Rome, and St. Paul argued that all government is ordained of God. Jesus and Paul labored indefatigably to change the lives of people so that their association would be the common denominator upon which a free and righteous government could stand. The foundations of government in America were laid down through the genius of the Christian religion. While all those who participated in the founding did not belong to the church, it was, nevertheless, the belief in each other and in the power of God to rule their lives and to lead them in the establishment of a just society, which inspired them. It was God, not themselves, who established the rights of man which all were bound to respect. Theirs was a religious problem, and they sought to evolve a religious answer to it. It was the genius of Christianity which released men from their fears, gave meaning and purpose to their lives, taught them that they were children of God, and gave them a sense of responsibility to God for their world, enlightened their conscience that they might know their complicity in the tragedies and the failures of their time, and fired their spirits to quest for a society in which man could achieve what God hoped for, for man, and what man desired for himself.

Democracy comes from the heart of committed and dedicated individuals. Democracy is the ultimate contribution of all men, both as creatures of and co-workers with God, in the unfinished task of achieving a better world. It takes no less to defend, improve, and extend the high ideals of this basically religious principle of government today than it did when the Pilgrim Fathers laid the foundation for it over three hundred years ago.

Of the thirteen colonies, five were under religious rule: the Pilgrims and Puritans in New England; the Covenanters in New Jersey; the Quakers in Pennsylvania; the Roman Catholics in Maryland; the Huguenots in the Carolinas. Through all the Colonies, and throughout our history, devoted adherents to Judaism played a vital and significant religious role in the building of the nation. The founding fathers laid the foundation firmly, after seeking the guidance and the help of God. "Then conquer we must for our cause it is just, and this be our motto, 'In God is our trust!' "

An appeal to Christian ministers and laymen to take a vital interest in politics is in no way to be interpreted as argument against the historical principle of the separation of Church and State—a principle our people established because of the sad experience and internal conflict which vexed Europeans from the fifth to the nineteenth centuries. The same conflicts got a foothold on these shores at first, and we had to dig them out root and branch in the early days of our history. What is meant by separation of Church and State does not mean that we want a godless government any more than did Jesus or Paul. Nor do we want a political method divorced from moral presuppositions. Rather do we mean that there shall be no organic relationship between Church and State; that no religious test shall ever be required as qualification for an office of public trust; that Congress shall make no law respecting an established religion, or prohibit the free exercise of any religion; that no religious body shall have preferential treatment, or access to the public funds to support its work; and that, on the other hand, no religious body shall dictate to the government.

The fulfillment of the dream of the true democratic society is something hoped for, but not quite attained. And though not yet attained, men believe it is entirely possible. But we do not despair of it, because the pursuit always brings us closer to a fuller realization. And so we strive to fulfill the destiny of freedom by a continuous adjustment to reality, which constitutes the mainspring of a free society. Sometimes—because we are human—the failures have been miserable; sometimes we have almost lost freedom through neglect or carelessness; some of our citizens have tried to sell it; others have tried to appropriate it for themselves. But always we have fought for it tenaciously, willing to wade through seas of human blood, sweat, and tears.

Nor has this freedom of a democratic way of life always meant the same thing to everyone. The American dream—as we commonly refer to it, although this is but a particularization of the larger dreams of freedom which the whole world shares—has meant different things to different segments of the population. Archibald MacLeish pointed this fact up with great precision in a speech at the Freedom Forum:

Sometimes we seem to mean no more than a place on the earth's surface; sometimes a particular religious or economic system; sometimes things the way they are; sometimes things the way they used to be before the income tax, or during the Nineteen-Twenties, or, in any event, before Franklin Roosevelt. But it was none of these things—not even the last—that the word *America* meant when it changed the history of the world. Men did not love that word—America—they did not cross the sea to find it because it stood for a particular faith, or a particular way of doing business, or a particular parcel of earth, or a particular moment in time. Men loved it and followed it because it meant none of these things: because it meant indeed precisely the opposite of all of them.[4]

And this was because it meant more than all of them taken together. No matter how we differed and how far some men fell below its loftiest concepts, we—all of us—knew that our inherent rights were based upon a moral law which could not forever be flouted, and that our basic rights were written, in fact, into the fabric of the Constitution. When injustices were perpetrated against a citizen, he had two appeals for his protection and vindication: one to the majesty of the law, and the other to the religious conscience based on moral law and the will of God. It is this supreme quality within our democracy, this spiritual awareness of the dignity of man before God which, more than anything else, has unconsciously fired the imagination of the masses in Asia and Africa.

Our most crucial social, political, domestic, and international problems are still basically religious problems. Man may not be the product solely of his environment, but a bad environment reduces the chances of every man's achieving his God-given possibilities. In many cases—and our courts and penal institutions present abundant testimony of this—a wretched environment destroys God's greatest creation, man. God does not change the environment, but He does put noble motives and burning desires in the heart of men to change that environment so that His Kingdom may come to earth. Indeed, it is hard to conceive of personal salvation apart from social salvation.

When we speak of the rights of minorities, the worth of persons, a concern for the poor, the care of the sick and aged, the need for more equitable laws and a just society, and the elimination of waste and corruption, we are using moral and religious terminology. When we are dissatisfied with what we are, and the level which our society has attained in the light of what we believe and what we ought to and can be; when we ask how we can improve our society; and when we work for security for the people of our city, state, or nation, we are unconsciously giving witness to the underlying religious basis of life. We take our stand, not because something is good, but because it is altogether right, and because man is a being of unique worth in the sight of God. Rightness in itself connotes an orientation to an all-controlling power, above and beyond ourselves, whose pre-established harmony is so evident among the planets that we seek to establish that harmony as the basis of the most peaceful, secure, and human order.

It is most difficult, if not altogether impossible, to think of a single great advancement in enlightened government or social progress on the American scene which did not arise out of a profound religious inspiration. The Point Four Program of Technical Assistance to the underdeveloped areas of the earth was sold to former President Truman by two great Christians, Horace Holmes, a layman and agricultural expert from Tennessee, and Frank Laubach, a missionary. When our nation became a sanctuary for the oppressed and a haven for the homeless, it did so out of the religious conviction of the great and equal worth of all men as sons of God. Walter Horton has said: "The very heart and soul of every healthy civilization is to be found in its religion."

Democracy has never been what all men say it is, and it has never been as complete as many of us have hoped it would be. In spite of its failures, it remains the system of government most conducive to the best interests of God's creatures here on earth. Democracy is not the Kingdom of God, and the Church has never thought of it as synonymous with the Kingdom of God. Nevertheless, it is better than the systems initiated by the men who despise it and who put less trust in the human individual than God puts in him.

The preacher of the gospel in these disturbing times must preach the preservation of our nation, based as it is upon the high concepts of our Judaeo-Christian heritage. But our democratic society does not exist in a vacuum. Rather it is in and of the world. The preacher preaches, like the prophets of old, to sustain and preserve the religious basis of our society which must always be judged by Christian idealism, although the actuality seldom approximates the ideal. Then he must do more. He must help guide people to the methods best in keeping with the moral law by which a democratic society obtains its working principles.

Herein lies one of the grave dangers of our day. For our political society stands beleaguered against the ideology of militant communism. Communism, in the wilderness of international despair, is like the devil importuning Jesus in the wilderness of decision. Because our political institution has worked so well and is so much more wholesome and so much better than any other yet devised, we are tempted to idolize it. The "idolatry of the democratic process" and the "deification of the concept of free enterprise"—as though they were the mainspring of the Kingdom of God, which would perish if they perished—is as dangerous as any other idolatry. Under some circumstances, it can be more dangerous than other idolatries, especially if and when we try to make an instrument out of God to serve the end of the nation, the economic or social system, or the nation's struggle. The state, the church, and even the preacher, are instruments of God.

Within our lifetime, most of us have witnessed the terrible rise of this attitude in our country. In the not-too-distant past—(a year or so ago can be called the past considering the galloping pace of historical forces)—we sustained a series of rude shocks to our freedom, and had to rise to guard that freedom against demagogues within the nation. Any responsible citizen who opposed such threats to our freedom from within, and who in devotion to his country spoke out as his conscience dictated, found himself vilified by those who elected to set themselves up as the final authority on a man's loyalty to his country.

What idealism but the religion of Jesus, what institution but the Church of our Lord Jesus Christ, what voices but the voice of the minister of Christ, can save us from false patriotism, which so readily leads to a perversion of freedom?

It has always been the historic mission of the Church to be the conscience of the political order and the "leaven" of the social order. The Church has been the constant reminder to governments that God passes judgment on man's achievements—even his best achievements, since God's judgment is higher than man's. It remains the one witness which keeps statesmen, government officials and politicians conscious, even when they ignore the fact, that they are held accountable for their actions to a higher law than they can legislate. This was the message and the work of the prophets, and it is inextricably interwoven all through the pages of the Old Testament and reiterated constantly in the New Testament. The Protestant witness has at least one foot in the prophetic tradition.

But it is not enough for the preacher in this day to limit himself to an appeal to the Christian conscience and to the Church as a "leaven"—a social solvent as it were—to be applied to the political problems and issues. He has an obligation to deal with the more practical problems and methods of how citizens reach the high goal of the democratic way of life, and how they obtain political power to reach that goal. To do this, the minister need not, and should not, devote himself to partisan politics in the pulpit, for reasons that are obvious. He can do it most effectively by applying the great truths of religion to the problems of society and government as he preaches throughout the year. He can do it by leading his congregation to the deeper inspection of and introspection on the basis of government and its relationship to ethics and religion. He can do it by communicating his own deep interest in whatever concerns the happiness and the welfare of God's children, and by kindling an enthusiasm for corporate responsibility in the minds of his congregation. And he can do it by patiently helping his people in quiet, unhurried ways to understand that politics, by means of which government is organized and directed, is not something outside religion.

To be sure, no matter how lovingly and how skillfully a minister works to make his communicants aware of their responsibilities, he will meet difficulties with some of the more fanatical members of the church who have completely ignored the fact that our democratic society is the product of the Protestant witness. Some things have to be endured, and some calculated risks have to be taken, but we must stand by our convictions with courage and express them with love. This may be difficult to do, but it is possible to do it. Moreover, it often wins converts to our position, and more often obtains a sympathetic hearing.

Even a cursory experience with politics at the grass-roots level is disturbing to a Christian. An excursion into it, at almost any level, is discouraging and is often so repulsive that it makes a great many of us turn our backs upon it. Here again, some things have to be endured, fought out, changed. Life is like that. Staying outside or running away is no answer. You have to stand up to life. You have to stand up for the Church. You have to stand up against Communism. You have to stand up against evil and tyranny. And you have to stand up for democracy and redeem it from political corruption. It is our country, our way, our future, our freedom. But only devoted religious people and consecrated religious leaders are ever going to redeem and reclaim it.

It is of course true that there is little idealism in much of our politics, and that a great number of people work at it and eventually enter government service for selfish motives which have little or no relation to the common good. But it is also true, as I have recently observed through my personal experience with politics and political campaigns, that men and women can mask their real motives in the intensity of a political campaign less effectively than in almost any other area of action. And I have known some men and women who have a positive, creative, and wholesome impact on politics and politicians. The trouble is that there are so few men and women who will pay the price to work at politics.

Like anything else of value and worth, it demands its price. It costs something to achieve good government. It costs the time and ability of the ablest, most sincere and unselfish citizens.

I doubt seriously, however, that pastors active in a parish ministry should hold public office unless they take a leave of absence from the church while doing so. Any other course, it seems to me, would do a great injustice to society and an even greater injustice to the church. It is open to serious question whether a clergyman under any condition should stand for public election.

I say this because I ran for office once. I am sure the motive for my decision to run was a good one—to interest Christians in government at the level where they can achieve most for their efforts, the grass-roots. It is at this point that the professional politician and the corrupt official obtain their great advantage over the rest of us. Moreover, I was protesting the undemocratic method of one great religious body and of one political party in limiting the nomination of candidates to one religious group—a policy which I am sure is unhealthy in a democratic society. I abhorred the selection of candidates on the basis of race, religion, and creed.

On the other hand, I am sure the decision to run for office was not a wise one, and I would never do it again nor advise any other clergyman to do so. Rather, it should be the religious leader's duty to help set the high moral standards by which all acts of government will be measured. For "Righteousness exalteth a nation, but sin is a reproach to any people." At the very least, the responsibility of a religious leader, or a religious institution, is to encourage men and women of integrity and idealism to enter the arena of politics and government and to enlighten their constituencies on the issues of the day. Edmund Burke, the great English statesman, put the problem succinctly for us when he said, "When bad men combine, the good must associate."

Even in this respect, Protestants fail rather miserably. When I ran for Borough President of Manhattan in 1953, only five Protestant churches and three ministerial organizations invited me to address them. I did not ask for the opportunity to speak from their *pulpits*, but rather for the opportunity to speak to groups in the social rooms. At no time during the campaign did I speak about my candidacy from my own pulpit, and I held no political rallies in the church. But surprisingly, fifty-seven rabbis, and even more surprisingly, one Roman Catholic priest, invited me to speak to groups in their basements or social rooms.

While I strongly advocate intelligent political action and preaching on the part of the minister, he should nevertheless be aware of the dangers which beset him, and which he should studiously avoid. There is, first of all, the danger of over-simplification of issues and problems; second, the naive confidence we too often have in ourselves, our judgment, the methods we use, and the parties we may be inclined to support. There is the danger of becoming too identified even with a good cause, and in this way we may lose our objective Christian criticism of all causes and movements, including the one in which we believe.

John Bennett, professor at Union Seminary, has wisely warned that interest in a political problem can become more decisive for us, if we let it, then our allegiance to the gospel, or to the Church. The prophets of Israel are good guides for the modern preacher in this respect. They never became so identified with the nation, the government, or even the religious order, that they could not view them from the point of view of God's eternal judgment.

A clergyman must always be in a position to criticize the movements and efforts of political action which he supports as a citizen. This is both his right and his responsibility, because the method of government we love, seek to improve, and preserve, is an achievement through the tortures and hazards of political organization and action. He should keep the interest of the people foremost. Every minister should scrupulously avoid taking unfair advantage of the communicants, consciously or unconsciously. He should provide opportunity and a logical setting for full and free participation in discussion, and for give and take, which is after all the genius of democracy.

Because I have led many delegations of social workers, ministers, civic leaders, and business executives to hearings and appointments with city councilmen, legislators, mayors, and governors, on a variety of protests, issues, and causes, one fact has become painfully apparent to me: that officials almost always looked up the voting record of the area we represented before we arrived at their offices. They had no way of knowing how the individuals of the area voted, but they wanted to see how seriously the people of that area took their responsibility. If the area had a low proportional voting record in relation to the rest of the city, the officials in question usually gave us a hard time, regardless of the justice of our cause. I regret to say that Harlem—the area of New York City in which I live and work—does not come off well in this regard. As a consequence, rightly or wrongly, we suffer greatly. And this is partly the fault of Harlem citizens.

Above all, it is the minister's duty to help citizens to understand the practical workings of politics and to teach them how to make good influences felt, and how to develop political strategy. Few clergymen understand that the lowly ward leader often has more influence with a mayor, governor or legislator than they do. Again, few civic, business, and religious leaders understand another relatively simple fact: that the workers of political parties—especially if the party is in power—can be exceptionally helpful in getting problems and issues before the proper authority. There are many common sense ways and means of politics that ministers ought to know and help their people to understand. One other fact often lost sight of is this: the political leader on every level is a human being. He can be reached through consideration as a person and through love. He can be cultivated and influenced if he is treated as a child of God, which he is, and not as an outcast, to be tolerated as a necessary evil, which he is not.

The privilege of the ballot is so great in a free society that it becomes almost a sacred obligation to the citizens. Moreover, it is rooted in the precious religious heritage of our Judaeo-Christian theology which stresses the ultimate and equal worth of all persons in the sight of God. Or, to put it another way, each man is an end in himself to the glory of God, not merely a means to an end for some other reason. Unhappily, too large a section of our citizens take lightly the privilege and obligation of the ballot. Many never bother to vote, and of those who do, far too few vote in the primary elections. Campaigns are costly and therefore susceptible to the influence of those who have money for ulterior motives, since all kinds of gimmicks must be employed to arouse the citizens to do what is necessary in order to preserve their liberties and to govern themselves.

A mistaken notion is widely current in our time among those who *are* enough concerned to vote. It is the fallacious assumption that a citizen does his full duty when he votes in the general election. Most do not bother with the primary election at all, although this is the place where one can pass upon the fitness of candidates. All we can do in the general election is to make a limited choice among candidates previously picked for us by an even more limited group to whom the candidates have probably made commitments, not always in the public interest. An even more important place where citizens can exert decisive influence is at the grass-roots level of the district organization, or—to use an abused but more realistic term—the district clubhouse. It is at this level that our ablest and finest Christian people should be co-workers.

It is not too much to hope for a time in America when every school child, every high school and college youth, will have the opportunity to take courses in practical politics, as well as in civics and government, when churches through regular programs and summer conferences for youths and adults will lead their numbers to a higher religious conception of secular government, when men and women will really learn how to split their vote to make their choice on the fitness of the candidate and not vote blindly for the party machine, when they will not be swayed unduly by emotions, when voters will give at least as much attention to constitutional amendments and other such matters as they do to the candidates, when citizens will so conduct their political machinery that the politician will no longer be an enigma, and when the finest and most cultured and worthy among us will count it an honor and a privilege to work at the level of the clubhouse.

It is not too much to hope that the creative genius of a nation which, with God's guidance, purchased our free society with the sacrifice and blood of devout men and women, will re-purchase the machinery through which new vision, heightened concern, and righteous motivation can control government.

We desperately need a righteous basis for our country in this hour of world crisis when millions have lost their freedom, and when even our freedom is in great jeopardy. God expects much from every one of us, and most certainly He expects each of us to apply His righteous will toward everything which affects the happiness, dignity and security of our society.

VI

THE INCLUSIVENESS OF THE
WORD MADE FLESH

THE gospel of Christ is the good news of God, sovereign over
all things, breaking in upon our world. It requires a preaching
rich in adventurous thought, including all aspects of life and
relating them directly to the supreme adventure of the "Word
made flesh."

Truly dynamic preaching is just that: demonstrating how God
is ever revealing Himself through Christ to us, whoever and
wherever we are; showing how He is ever meeting us in our
human situations, since He took our nature upon Himself. If you
encounter Him, there is no room for evasive excuses, nor for
vague reasons why you cannot follow Him, nor for reservations
why you cannot present Him as the truth to others. You cannot be
neutral. And if you could, it would not be an honorable position.
You have to make up your mind because there is no middle ground.
"He that is not with me is against me." But if you "come and follow me I will make you fishers of men."

In his book, *The Plight of Freedom*, Dr. Paul Scherer writes:

> Whatever else you may say of such a gospel, you cannot call it irrelevant. Its very character as personal encounter in a personal world between persons and one Person whose Being is contingent upon no other, establishes it as the primal source and spring of freedom. In no other context can human life recover and maintain the essential dignity of its own selfhood . . . In no other context and on no other basis can that relationship be wrought out between man and man which must provide the pattern of the future, if the future is to be liveable and existence to be meaningful again.[1]

But with all the potential power of God, the eternal presence of Jesus right at hand—"Lo, I am with you always even unto the end of the world"—with all his words in the gospel, such as, "Go ye unto all the world and make disciples of all men," we still see too many preachers limiting themselves to particular kinds of people, and then torturing their minds to find some flimsy, meaningless excuse to justify themselves.

To be sure, men have different talents and abilities, but any man who accepts the call of God should be willing and able to proclaim that message of the living word to all.

Too easy a distinction is made between the minister at home and the missionary abroad. Are we not all called "to endure hardship as good soldiers"? Too many seminary students set their hopes early on the larger "successful and famous churches," whatever that means. I doubt that it means, in the context of Jesus, that a Fifth Avenue church or my own church is more Christian than a rude building lost on the wide prairies in the expansive Midwest, or a small log cabin in the mountains of West Virginia—not, in any event, so long as devout folk gather there to encounter the grace and glory of God. The United Church of Canada perhaps understands St. Paul better than some of us south of the border when it demands that seminary graduates give a year or so up in the lumber camps of the north, or on the bleak coast of Nova Scotia, before it will ordain them. Our sister church up there encourages its clergy to have an inclusive encounter with men of every condition and walk of life.

Even the pagan founder of a Greek mystery cult, Pythagoras, saw the necessity of making his philosophy embrace all men. He resolutely insisted that his disciples—and at one time he is said to have had six hundred—be able to communicate their system to any man who would listen. His desire to reach all was so inclusive that he did something which it took Christians eighteen centuries to do: he admitted women to the higher education of his day five hundred years before the Christian era. Surely the Christian minister as a disciple of Jesus has a higher and a brighter star to guide him than had Pythagoras' disciples.

There is a natural enough tendency toward specialization in our world today, and much of this has both directly and indirectly affected the ministry of the Church. Some such borrowing from the worlds of business and science is good, for it is in keeping with the growth of the Church in an ever-expanding society. The increase of knowledge, both of the world of nature and the nature of man, demands new techniques and new specialists to apply the techniques. Religious methods try to keep a fairly even pace with the general progress, and consequently the Church needs and demands experts. There can be no quarrel with this. But I suggest that consecrated laymen, rather than preachers, should be trained as the specialists since a preacher's task is already a highly special one.

Preachers are called to an inclusive task of winning souls and improving converts. We all have different talents in one direction or another, and these are but tools to effect a finer craftsmanship in the art of our calling.

My concern is rather for those of us in the ministry who become spokesmen for particular groups—and examples of this sort are far too numerous for a robust church and a healthy religion. It is not easy for us to acknowledge that much of our preaching and our orientation reflects the unconscious compromise we have made to our surroundings. But when we honestly face ourselves in the fragile mirror of our time, we see that every preacher in the land runs the same risks.

It is as easy for the minister in the suburbs to succumb to temptation and constitute himself the defender of the more fortunate, as it is for the minister in the slums to fall into the error of being the champion of the poor. It is not difficult to become the advocate of labor if your heart and your work are among those who toil with their hands; and even less difficult, perhaps, to become the darling of the National Association of Manufacturers. All of us have seen tragic examples of ministers to "white churches" who find it difficult to invite a Negro into their pulpit, even on the Sunday which marks race-relations day each year, and who are even more uncomfortable, awkward, and naively apologetic when they are invited to preach in a "Negro church." And I well remember an outstanding clergyman of great fame who once told the white associate of a Negro pastor that he ought not remain with that church so long that his white brethren came to think of him as "one who ministered solely to Negroes." Some clergymen and mission board secretaries cannot see any contradiction between the call for men to go out into all the world, and a refusal to apply the same call to similar situations at home.

It is equally difficult for many Negro preachers to preach to a "white congregation." They are tempted to assume a superior righteousness when they address a group of those who have sinned against their race. Every Negro knows the insidious urge to pour the venom of contempt upon a white congregation when the opportunity presents itself. Few have escaped either the temptation or the dubious satisfaction of strewing a few prickly barbs in their sermons.

There is something tragically pathetic in Negro ministers who hold tenaciously to the Negro church because they believe these places of segregated worship are their only guarantee of religious leadership. And something equally pathetic is the anemic claim of white ministers who plead that 'the time is not right' for racial integration in the Church of Christ. It is not unreasonable to believe that both put more trust in the evil of men than they do in the power of God. To those who resist the gospel message, the time is never right; and to those who permit social ostracism and discrimination, the time has long since passed for a change of circumstances. Good men striving for a righteous and just order of human relations *make* the time right.

One September, I conducted a week of preaching services to several hundred young Texans who, with the exception of three or four, were white. A Negro pastor afterwards told me, "I just couldn't do that. I think I'd know what to say, but I wouldn't know how to say it. How can you take the liberty down here in the South of saying what you say so boldly? They don't even seem to take offense!" There is only one answer: helping people face the encounter of truth in love. I did not see white Texans sitting before me . . . I only saw human beings seeking an encounter with God, and I was but His agent.

To the consternation of both whites and Negroes, a young white pastor, Arthur Ormant of Westminister Presbyterian church—who has lived, studied, and worked in the South all of his life—invited me to preach at his church in Tuscaloosa, Alabama. Several Negro pastors urged me to refuse the invitation as too dangerous. "Besides," as one of them said, "you'll just be wasting your time. Nothing's going to change them." I assume he meant that not even God could change attitudes of prejudice.

Some of Pastor Ormant's elders were also opposed to the idea. Even I had said, when he first asked me to preach, "If you had made this request over the phone, I'd have asked you if you really knew who I was." To which he replied, "I know not only who you are, but I know something else—you'll be leaving Monday morning, and I'll have to stay here."

When he introduced me that morning, he said simply, but with strength mingled with love, "The Protestant Church stands in the tradition of a prophetic ministry. I have been listening to the Reverend Robinson preach all week over at Stillman Institute. I felt that what he had to say was so important that you would not think me a good pastor if I did not invite him to this pulpit." That was all—no apologies, and no softening-up tactics.

Three incidents—among others—stand out in my memory, as I look back on that occasion. I stood at the door greeting the people with Pastor Ormant. A young man said, as he took my hand in both of his, "My only regret is that I'm twenty-two, and that this is the first time I have heard the word of God from the lips of a Negro minister in a church like this. That is twenty-two years too late, but I'm glad I was here this morning." An elderly lady said gently, "Young man, I am eighty-five and my father held slaves. If you could have preached to him as you preached to me this morning, he would have given those slaves their freedom." A distinguished gentleman, who announced himself as the Dean of the School of Business and Commerce and Acting President of the University of Alabama, told me, "I don't belong to this church, and I gather that a great many who were here this morning do not belong here either. I belong to the First Presbyterian church downtown. I don't think we'd have have had the courage to have asked you to preach in our church. Someone called me last night and told me there was a revolution in town, and when they told me what it was, I told them I wanted to be part of that kind of a revolution."

When Pastor Ormant saw me off at the airport the next afternoon, he told me that he had received thirty-seven calls of commendation, and none of condemnation. I am not to judge, but it seems hardly human if some did not condemn privately, or *sotto voce*. The great point, however, is that when those who wished to condemn encountered the new-old demands of Jesus, they measured the place where they stood with the place to which he called them, and they could not refuse publicly to do his bidding. This was, at least, a good beginning. If we do not at least begin, we shall never move upward and onward.

It is a fallacious assumption that a true exponent of the gospel, who has the spirit of Christ, the love of God, the knowledge of man, and just average intelligence, cannot preach to one as to all. All men have fears from which they want release. All men are disturbed by the same imponderable problems of life for which they seek answers.

What is the meaning of the universe? Does my life have a pur-

pose? Why am I *here?* All men desire to be loved and want someone to receive that love and return it in full measure—not
greedily but because it establishes their worth as persons. This is
not the love of the body, which often becomes enslavement, but
the love of the spirit, which becomes a sacrament. All men know
that they are morally incapable and are moved by emotional folly
and incredible weakness of will. The answers to these yearnings
are no different for one man than for another. Even my forefathers
in the dark and ignorant days of slavery knew that: they sang in a
spiritual, "If religion was a thing that money could buy, the rich
would live and the poor would die."

A group of prep-school lads, led by a boy in the Fourth Form,
waited on me in the living room of Headmaster Saltonstall's house
after morning chapel when I preached at Exeter one Sunday.
When I asked them what they wanted to see me about, the
leader spoke up.

"Nothing," he said, "we came to thank you for preaching the
gospel to us. We needed that, and we wanted it. So many ministers
who come to Exeter talk to us about philosophy, science, or literature, and only a little about religion. I guess it's because they think
that since this is a famous school and some of us have wealth and
privilege, we are different. But we thank you for preaching the
gospel about what we should do with our lives for God's sake."

He was right, for the spiritual needs of teen-age boys are the
same, whether they are on the Lower East Side or in the most
exclusive prep school. Neither group may recognize it, but they
have common needs, if not common problems. Some of the most
unhappy youth come from homes of great privilege. It is to be
seriously doubted that a school or college pastor ought to undertake the task of ministering to youth until he has had a broad and
solid pastoral ministry. Children may be out of their homes, but
they are not out of life's context.

The preaching of some ministers lacks inclusiveness because
they project their own basic need as the sole need of others. All
men have in some measure the same basic needs, but these vary
according to the given place and time. Even if the congregation

should be of the same race, at the same cultural level, or in the same economic group, their needs would be as varied as the individuals themselves.

Not infrequently, the preacher plants the seeds of his message in one narrow furrow because he was captivated in seminary—or even after seminary days—by an intellectual giant whom he seeks to emulate. Therefore, he may ride a lopsided hobby—a particular theological system, the social gospel, international problems, or psychiatric theories, in which he often becomes more of a menace than a help—to the exclusion of the varied diet necessary to feed the hungry sheep of the Kingdom. There are enough, if not too many, pseudo-psychiatrists in the ministry who parrot platitudes about a nebulous positivism of the mind as the method of escape from pain, failure, difficulties, and suffering. Joy comes through sorrow, peace out of strife; fulfillment comes through hunger, the birth of a baby comes through pain. The life of a Christian comes out of the death of Christ; the life of every new idea is conceived in discomfiture, fathered by resistance, mothered by pain, and grows through torture.

One of the greatest needs of our world now, is—and always has been—fellowship with God beyond the barriers. The minister's supreme task is to lead men and women into Christ's divinely appointed fellowship of the Church and to arouse them against the enemy which is common to society and to themselves. The minister's task is to help all men see that beyond all natural help at their disposal they need the divine aid of God. George Adam Smith was one of the most brilliant of Biblical scholars, but he remained an elder in a humble mission church in the less fortunate section in Glasgow and preached without rancor or bitterness to the great and mighty of the fashionable churches of Scotland. Was it not St. Paul, of whom King Agrippa said, "Almost thou persuadest me," who won and received Onesimus, the slave, into the Church by his witness of the inclusive word?

Every minister knows the danger of becoming a false prophet. Such a man keeps his popularity by becoming a mere propagandist. Unhappily, there are not a few among us who pander to the prejudices and whims of people and the currents of the time. It is only right to add that while some of us do this, we are, nevertheless, remorseful because of our inability to overcome it. In the end, such ministers reap nothing more than the contempt of those to whom they sold themselves too cheaply—and the condemnation of God, who anointed them.

There are still Ahabs to rage, "There is yet one man, Micaiah the son of Imlah, by whom we may inquire of the Lord: but I hate him, for he doth not prophesy good concerning me." (I KINGS 22:8) And there are still Zedekiahs who willingly do Ahab's bidding and urge Micaiah to change the message and "prophesy" flattering phrases to frivolous minds. When the preacher stands firm, we metaphorically smite him, as Zedekiah did Micaiah, and cast him into prison. But Ahab was so sure that Micaiah was the real prophet —and that his "mouthpiece," Zedekiah, was not even a suitable substitute for the real thing—that he disguised himself to evade the judgment of God when he rode out to battle. But that did not save him. The judgment of God caught up with Ahab and he perished.

The basic difficulties and the fundamental problems which face all men are the same. All men, despite differences of race, station, education, or geography, "have sinned and fallen short of the glory of God." Some of us have been more sinned against than others, but all of us are sinners in need of redemption. There are Negroes who are as prejudiced as "dyed in the wool" Southern whites. Labor leaders are often as ruthless as "robber barons." Gracious ladies—by the standards of the society page—are sometimes as morally loose as the misguided girl in the slums. Both are influenced by an age which emphasizes physical satisfaction to the neglect of the deeper dimensions of human love. There may be different degrees of cheating, prejudice, hate, thievery, cruelty, dishonesty, lust, pride, injustice, and vanity, but it is the fact of the evil, not the degree, with which God is concerned.

Howsoever men may differ in culture, economic circumstances, racial origin, or intellectual development, all are but fallible beings in need of God's grace and redemption. There is not one degree of sin for a Negro or a poor man, and another for a Jew, a

Gentile, or a rich man. Jesus says, "Come unto me all ye who are heavy laden." He speaks of the same burden of care, anxiety, frustration, disappointment, failure, unfulfilled hopes, broken hearts, sin. The burden of the rich man's money bags is often no heavier than that of the poor man's debts.

All men as psychological beings need discipline for their lives if the baser instincts, which survive our ancient animal heritage, are to be subdued. All men need to practice the art of living justly, honestly, and lovingly, within their several groups, and in society at large. There is no difference when a rich man lacks an understanding of the true dimensions of his existence, and when a poor man does. The president of the Ladies' Aid—and what pastor has not had this experience—can be as obstinately self-centered as the scholar who seeks for what he calls "objective truth" and sets himself against the positions held by all others. Man's interest in himself as the center of the universe is an obsession to which most of us are addicted. The preacher never lacks opportunity for challenging men and women to "get rid of too much *me*." The genius of religion and of life by which a man finds direction, happiness, and purpose is the same for all, as indeed is the power by which each and all of us are sustained in our adversities. As ministers, we are to preach the gospel to all alike, even when their interests are in conflict.

Man needs the glory of God's light on his pathway. Nothing but the glory of God can satisfy the hunger of his soul and relieve him of his surging doubts and quench his tantalizing temptations to flaunt the will of God. Inherent in the grace of God—and we cannot repeat this too often—is the pain and suffering which flows through contrition. This, too, is alike for all mortal flesh, since Christianity is the religion of the cross—"a cross for everyone and there is a cross for me." It was borne by Jesus, but it pierced the heart of God as it tore the shackles of sin away from our lives.

There is pain in torn flesh and crushed pride. Every moral advance has its price tag. It costs something, but the cost purchases a joy past understanding. That joy, too, is free to all. "Whosoever will, let him come." By the same inevitable consequence of sin-

ful acts, all men need the redeeming grace of God's forgiveness
to achieve salvation. The forgiveness for Pilate, for members of
the Sanhedrin, and for the Roman soldiers was the same as that for
the thief. The only difference is that the thief asked for it and
the others did not. It is any man's for the asking, the acceptance,
and the living. "God is no respecter of persons." (ACTS 10:34)

In the "hour of transition," as Longfellow calls the occasion of
passing from this life to the life beyond, the industrial tycoon
stands just as alone before the judgment seat as the debt-ridden
ditch digger. They are equally at the mercy of God, and without
any valid advocate save Christ Jesus. There is only one possible
hope for them, and it cannot be bought by the wealth of the
former, nor borrowed by the begging of the latter. It can be
merited, however, by both, for they have an equal chance to prepare for that hour which the poet John Keats described in the
lines of a sonnet:

> When I have fears that I may cease to be . . .
> . . . . then on the shore
> Of the wide world I stand alone, and think,
> Till Love and Fame to nothingness do sink.

Every man stands in the judgment alone. As my grandfather used
to say, "Every tub stands on its own bottom."

The minister preaches the adventure of faith to all alike. John
Knox, standing trial before Mary Queen of Scots, is reported to
have said, "I have never feared a face of common clay, even
though it be a Queen's." Knox took St. Paul seriously when the
Apostle explained his call to the church at Ephesus in these words:

> Whereof I was made a minister, according to the gift
> of the grace of God given unto me by the effectual
> working of his power . . . that I should preach among the
> Gentiles the unsearchable riches of Christ, And to make
> all men see what is the fellowship of the mystery, which
> from the beginning of the world hath been hid in God.
> (EPHESIANS 3:7–9)

We must adventure with St. Paul in those regions where no man is so commonplace that he cannot be a prince in the Kingdom of Heaven.

Some years ago, the elders and deacons in the church I serve decided to conduct a revival. Although our planning and preparation studiously avoided the side-show effects of "storming the fortress of sin," we unequivocally determined upon an evangelism of enthusiastic witnessing by laymen, and preaching by pastors who would demand personal decisions and promises. A fellow member of our denomination asked me to let him know the success of such archaic methods—that if perchance we succeeded, he might try it in his parish.

We decided to conduct a series of meetings for a whole week. For three months before the week of revival, a group of officers and members met weekly for training and prayer. A revival begins by strengthening the faithful. We laid hands upon our professionals, laborers, teachers, mail carriers, social workers, housewives, and young people, and sent them forth to minister unto the people in their group, profession, office, factory, and apartment houses, and to bring them to church at least once during that week.

Only three accessions were made by the end of that revival week, but in the follow-up by laymen during the next month, over forty were gained. Among them were politicians, social workers, a labor leader, lawyers, doctors, school teachers, and the neighborhood drunk—who to this day has remained steadfast. Most of them had never been baptized.

I remember well the social worker who came to me and asked to be relieved of her assignment because she did not know how to approach social workers in her office, trained as they were in a materialistic approach to the problems of personal and family distress. I suggested that she take her Bible to work and at lunch open it and read quietly to herself. I guaranteed her that curiosity would open the windows of conversation through which she could bear witness. It worked for her, as the grace of God worked through all of them who went forth to spread the gospel, for she had planted the title of Samuel Shoemaker's book in her heart, *Revive Thy Church Beginning With Me*.

God was pleased with the effort, because the doubtful were led to faith, the careless to concern, the lost to safety, the sinner to salvation, and we were not afraid to encourage the brightest, ablest, and most influential of our associates to devote themselves to the task of spiritual reconstruction. Nor did we hesitate to challenge the most sophisticated with the need to be lifted above themselves by the power and the help of God.

Our clergy asked no greater sacrifice of our laymen than we were willing to demand of ourselves. We undertook to do some street-corner preaching in the neighborhood. It would give every minister a wonderful blessing if he would occasionally engage the problem of sin out in the open where he does not have the support of liturgical surroundings, the vested choir at his back, the vestrymen and the deacon on his flanks, and the army of the faithful who, though seated respectfully before him, are often anxious to conclude the battle by the stroke of twelve, even though the salient may not have been breached as yet.

I tell you, it is a different thing out there in the cold, with the noise of the traffic whizzing by, with no captive audience to smile their approval politely back. With, instead, the impish, leering up to rattle you if they can. With the frowns of the respectable trying to make up their minds whether or not you are a fraud and whether the devil, who did not leave church at high noon last Sunday, has not followed you here. When you try hard to stop the first man hurrying home at the end of a hard day, or the woman rushing back to the store for something she forgot for supper, or the young people who are off to an evening of entertainment—and you succeed, *that* is adventurous preaching!

Standing out there with nothing but the help of God, which in the last analysis is all you need, is an experience every minister—especially every seminary student—should have. That is where St. Paul stood, and Wesley, and a host of others. That is where Jesus stood. Above all, that is where most of the people of the world are—out there; outside the Church, either as an institution or a fellowship.

The men and women today, the great bulk of them who need Christ, are not in churches at all. They are in factories, stores, and shops working six days a week and trying to do their shopping, cleaning, washing, ironing, resting, relaxing, and mending on the seventh; hounded by continual pressure for materialistic happiness via radio, newspapers, television, magazines and movies, in the form of "Queen for a Day," an air-conditioned home in the newest development, a Jaguar; and they are miserably unhappy because they know they will never get closer than a picture—in color, perhaps—of their dreams. They are hoboes along the religious highways sleeping in a wash under an Arizona winter moon; they are girls in strange cities trying to find jobs and wondering what they will do when they cannot find one, and threatening to commit suicide if no job turns up, or turning to easier, more sordid pursuits with respectable businessmen who have an eye for figures; they are disillusioned young people whose fathers and mothers, or aunts and uncles, made such a fetish of religion that it became a grim spectre to be avoided at all costs; they are the Ira Hayes of today, torn between an old culture and a new, of heroism on Iwo Jima and of dying alone and forgotten on an Indian reservation—and given a hero's funeral, with all its mock adulation, in Arlington cemetery.

They are lonely old women and old men trying to stretch their meager savings to last as long as they can in this time of increasing life expectancy, and haunted day and night by the fact that they will probably outlast the money. They are anemic little clerks who line the lunch counters of the nation at noontime, hastily swallowing their sandwich and coffee, with the person behind waiting for their seats, poking them in the back, or coughing over their shoulder trying to see how many more bites before they are finished. They are in concentration camps, or, if they are lucky enough, refugee camps. They are bewildered university students caught up for the first time, and far from the home shore, in the whirlpool of scientific humanism which will sweep them away like chips on the crest of a flood. They are in Communist countries, fear-bound-loyal to those who hold them enslaved, with no one to set them free.

They are in trailer camps and cotton-picker camps. They are in "saloons" and they are in "night spots," and always in desperate flight from themselves because they have not let God show them how to love themselves.

Sometimes, with all due reverence for the symbolism and the tradition and the holiness of sacred places like churches, I think it might be a good thing for churches *per se* to be destroyed, thus dispersing God's messengers to the four corners of the cities in which they live. This might force them to build their Holy Places, not by famous architects' plans and specifications, but by the strength of the message they can deliver on hilltops, street corners, windswept avenues, subway stations, railway terminals, and bus terminals. Here, of all places in the world, one would surely find those whom God is waiting to heal. But instead, like the lame man at the pool who could get no one to help him at the right time, those in want are being knocked aside by those in a hurry to catch the 5:15 for Greenwich, or the 4:49 for Glendale.

Preaching to such people would be an adventure—as indeed is all preaching which requires more than the turning of clever phrases; and by this I do not mean that we should be slovenly and not strive for creative expression in telling the good news. But if we become too clever with words, men will hang on to our phrases and forget to fall on their knees. Nothing is worth hanging to but a cross. Nothing. Our preaching should aim to exalt the inclusive Christ—not ourselves—and to strike straight to the root of human need. We should preach for a conviction today, and although the results may not appear until some tomorrow in the distance of the years, our responsibility is to do the best we can, and leave the results in the hands of God.

.   .   .   .   .

A bottle of water sealed with transparent tape arrived through the mail at my study some years ago. The single sentence printed on the wrapper intrigued me: "This bottle bears water from the Peace River of Northern Canada as a memorial for what you did for me seven years ago." No amount of excavation in my memory could uncover a clue. I pondered over the strange gift for a week.

A letter from the sender arrived a week later and cleared up the mystery. A part of it read as follows:

> I am neither a name nor a person to you, but the power of God changed my life through you. One cold February day you stood with your back to a fire speaking to students in the Student Christian Movement House at McGill University in Montreal. I came into the room for no other purpose than to get warm, but somehow I couldn't leave and missed my next class. I was a student of engineering, but what you said about the spiritual need of the Great Northwest so troubled and challenged me that I couldn't get it out of my mind, and you and God wouldn't let me go. I slipped out of the meeting without speaking to anyone. That seems long ago now, but here I am a minister to lumber camps. I am grateful to God that he sent you that day, and so I have sent you as a memorial of the occasion a bottle of water from the Peace River.

It is impossible to describe the joy and peace which that letter brought to my soul. I know now what St. Paul meant when he wrote in the eighth verse of the third chapter of Ephesians, "Unto me, who am less than the least of all saints, is this grace given, that I should preach among the Gentiles the unsearchable riches of Christ."

Our Lord Jesus Christ, about whom we preach, was the gift of God to all the world—"Whosoever believeth in him shall not perish, but have everlasting life"—and he addressed the needs of all the people of the earth. He was the friend of the sinner and the conscience of the saint; he succored the poor whom he greatly loved and rebuked the mighty whom he loved no less. He was the physician of the sick and the therapist for the mentally disturbed. He was the guide for the blind and the teacher of children. He was the savior of the penitent thief and the inspiration of the proud centurion. He was a Jew, but he converted Samaritans. He was the welcome guest in the home of the rich Nicodemus, but he also ate simple food in the crude huts of the publicans. He called fishermen, a tax gatherer, a political reformer to be his followers; and among the seventy must have been men of every station and walk of life. He sought to win the rich young ruler, whom he did not despise because he was rich, nor honor because he had money. He loved him for God's sake. We could learn a lesson here from Jesus. Many of us either damn the rich as oppressors or defer to them because of their wealth. Jesus did neither.

Bankers as ordinary men are no worse on the whole than labor leaders or the leaders of any other group. The Federal Examiner for the National Labor Relations Board had to rule against the Teamsters' Union of Oregon for practices unfair to some of its own employees early in 1955. During the latter part of 1954, David Dubinsky of the International Ladies' Garment Workers lodged an indignant but courteous protest with the Office Employee' International Union for calling a strike of the Garment Workers' office force without so much as informing Mr. Dubinsky before they gave the story to the newspapers.

And who do you think spoke the following words? A union leader? A minister? An industrialist?

> Christianity is not exciting and meaningful to thousands of Americans. But it ought to be. Whether life is superficial or wonderful, it is Christianity which makes the difference. Christianity to a business man will never make great strides until he begins to grasp the Gospel. We are still ashamed to talk about the eternal verities of the word of God. Too many people are reading books about the Bible and not enough are reading the Bible, too many are trying to make an ambulance-chaser out of God. Seek him now. Do not wait until trouble or sickness comes.

This was not a clergyman preaching. This was a banker from San Francisco, Arnold Gruigen, speaking to the annual banquet of the Christian Business Men's Committee in Tucson, Arizona. Would to goodness there were more ministers who would preach like this to laborers and business men alike.

We dare not associate ourselves with Jesus if we fail to proclaim an *inclusive* gospel of the word made flesh, a gospel which lives eternally and applies equally to the lives of all.

We who preach "are ambassadors for Christ" to the Kingdom of God. As an ambassador represents all the interests of his country and all the people of his nation, so do we under the authority of God represent all the interests of all the citizens of His Kingdom. All the interest God has in the world He has committed to His servants. If they fail in the discharge of responsibilities, His work is seriously handicapped. If the obligation is a weighty one, the opportunities for service are abundant, and the joy of being an agent of that living force which lifts men from the sordidness of sin to the presence of God is without comprehension. The prophets Nahum and Isaiah and the Apostle Paul all echo the supreme joy of the preacher in a thrilling passage:

> How beautiful are the feet of them that preach the gospel of peace, and bring glad tidings of good things! (ROMANS 10:15)

A preacher is more than a writer of sermons and a pastor of a congregation; he is the rung of a ladder from man to God and "a medium between the mind of God and the hearts of man." The Church is more than an association of imperfect people seeking redemption, and of moderately good people seeking betterment. It is an enduring fellowship created by God which binds man to man, and man to God. It embraces all men and crosses all boundaries. It stretches time into eternity, and its supreme task is to make men aware of their failures and sure of their hopes as they understand their need of God.

Such a preacher was Harry Emerson Fosdick, and such a church is the Riverside Church. No description of either is adequate to reproduce the dynamic impact of preacher or church, but I call them to your attention because they reflect, as nearly as any marriage of pastor and church, an example in which we rejoice in this difficult century.

The tower of the Riverside Church thrusts its blunt head high above the Manhattan skyline. When seen from the New Jersey shore of the majestic Hudson River, it seems to stand aloof even from the igneous rocks of Morningside Heights upon which it is anchored. Seen from the opposite direction, from the streets of Harlem, (crowded with three times as many people as the houses were built to accommodate), it is a lonely citadel sometimes so lost in the clouds that a red light warns low flying aircraft on a misty night.

On bright sunny days the long shadow cast by that mighty tower gently greets International House, the Jewish Theological Seminary of America, Columbia University, the Juilliard School, and Union Seminary—great institutions of knowledge, prestige, culture, influence, and power. And yet the shadow does not discriminate against the poverty of Manhattanville or the slums of Harlem. Indeed, the shadow integrates the fortunes and the lives of all under its spell, for it is not a tower to mark a point of separation on the surface of the earth, but a beacon in the sky pointing men from earth to the inclusiveness of heaven. Riverside, like many another church, could have isolated itself on that splendid and intellectual hill. There are ministers and churches, and we all know it, who are so exclusive that they merit the condemnation of the Apostle James:

> My brethren, show no partiality as you hold the faith of our Lord Jesus Christ, the Lord of glory. For if a man with gold rings and in fine clothing comes into your assembly, and a poor man in shabby clothing also comes in, and you pay attention to the one who wears the fine clothing and say, "Have a seat here, please," while you say to the poor man, "Stand there," or "Sit at my feet," have you not made distinctions among yourselves, and become judges with evil thoughts? . . . If you show partiality, you commit sin, and are convicted by the law as transgressors. (JAMES 2:1–4, 9)

But far beyond the farthest reaches of Riverside Church is the enduring influence of Dr. Harry Emerson Fosdick. Though pastor emeritus of one of the great churches of Christendom, he is a humble servant of the Lord, who preaches the inclusive word with such brilliance and clarity that on his lips it becomes flesh and dwells among us. Because it was the word of God alive in his heart, it came alive in that church and personified the oneness and the brotherhood of man, drawing God's children into a bond so natural that the laborer was at ease with the rich man in this church built by the Rockefellers, and the Negro lent more than color to the choir and assuagement to guilty consciences. The doors of its facilities were flung wide to the unhappy youth of various out-groups of other religious persuasions, and the membership became companions of distressed Irish, Puerto Ricans, Italians, and Negroes. The picture is not overdrawn, for the church has many problems to overcome, and much opposition from otherwise faithful men and women among the laity; and much growing need be done by the doubtful who always seem to find it hard to share their good fortune with the less fortunate. But the blessings outweigh the problems.

The fame of Riverside Church was the achievement of man, but the inspiration came from the great preacher, Fosdick, whose incisive message of the word of God to all men taught them to live, not by what they doubted or what they hated in others, but by what they believed about God and loved in themselves. Love of neighbor as love of self was not condemned by Jesus, but rather made the middle and higher step on the pathway to love of God. One never achieves proper other-love without proper self-love. Because Dr. Fosdick was not a special pleader for one group against another, no individual or group could claim property rights upon him as their spokesman. He preached—and lived by what he preached—a gospel which embraced all true Christian believers. A fellowship, if you please, magnificently capable of continuing Christ's mission on earth.

When he retired from his pastorate, he gave himself unstintingly to all people in every circumstance, again with the same compelling ability to reach their needs. He was always troubled because his duties of preaching and writing prohibited a more generous giving of himself to those on the fringes of the Heights. I once asked him to chair a benefit committee and help raise money for a Harlem Community Center. He accepted at once, and when we could find no other place to hold the meeting but a night club where the meeting had to be cut short in order to accommodate the night life patrons, he did not complain, although I suspect he was not happy about it. His presence illuminated that dingy room, and his speech made such an impression upon one of the waiters (a man, I may add, who had seldom been to church, had no faith and little formal education) that he gave me his wages for the night saying, "He makes everything so clear. I wish I had heard him years ago. That man has persuaded me. I've got to have a part in this work. Somehow, I want to be a better man. When can I come to talk to you?"

Here was adventurous preaching which took the uncertainty out of the way, and left in it the thrilling possibility of obtaining a nobler future both here and in the world to come . . . a future into which all men may adventure with confidence and hope.

VII

HOPE BEYOND DESPAIR

T HE most serious question of our time, in view of the fact that political, cultural, economic, and educational methods seem incapable of halting the crumbling of Western civilization, is: What can religion do?

Can it save the West? Can it halt disintegration of our society? Can it succeed where the science of technology and the forces of enlightened secularism have failed? Can it restore optimism and hope? Can it yet provide a secure foundation upon which we can build? These are hard-core questions today, and clergymen are looked to for the answers, since they represent the voice of the eternal in this transitory world.

Powerful forces at work in modern America are attempting to compress the richness of our cross-fertilized culture into a single mold, into a completely indigenous way of life. The Romans made this same mistake, admiring only themselves and what they called "Roman." As a result they reaped the dreary fruits of petrification. We are also creating debilitating idolatries. Some of them are obvious; some, like our idolatry of science, are doubly dangerous because of inherent perils unperceived at first glance. Many Americans have come to believe that man now has the same knowledge as God to create energy and rearrange matter. We seem to forget that man does not possess equal quantities of God's love, without which he can only annihilate himself and his world. Until God's grace and man's humility mitigate human sinfulness, man will continue to speak peace and wage war, will continue to be deceived by the heresy of Communism, which makes men do evil and speak of it as good, will continue to search for world peace in the forlorn and outmoded ways of international machinery, treaties, and power blocks, will continue to permit hysteria and fear to grip the mind so that men no longer trust each other, and redemption is no longer thought possible for those who once disagreed with the majority. Saddest of all, he will continue to express faith in everything but God, and the resulting tensions will show like earth-tremors on the seismographs of the human psyche.

Man has suffered famine, pestilence, war, and flood, but he has never experienced a time of such widespread anguish of heart and breakdown of mind. There is a violence in our world today which ravages the mind worse than any violence which crushes the body and destroys civilizations. The Reverend Henry Francis Lyte wrote in one of the lines of his famous hymn, *Abide With Me*, "Change and decay in all around I see."

Christian faith begins with faith in the eternal victory of God over the forces of decay, sin and evil. "Faith is not belief in spite of evidence," Kirsopp Lake once said, "but life in scorn of consequences." Elton Trueblood says, "Faith, as the plain man knows, is not belief without proof, but trust without reservation." John Henry Newman in his hymn, *Lead Kindly Light*, wrote, "One step by faith enough for me."

The preacher in every time of crisis and conflict must point people to religion's primary objective—an allegiance which is always above and beyond the present, and which challenges, judges, and redeems all human institutions and situations. The preacher must lead his congregation into an adventure of faith as Isaiah did when he cried, "Lift up your eyes on high, and behold who has created these things that bringeth out their hosts by number. He calleth them all by names by the greatness of his might, for he is strong in power. Not one faileth." For a time like this, we can be sustained by the faith that no possible combination of the powers of evil can permanently thwart the will of God.

The preacher, in times of earth-shaking events, is called upon to help people stand fast and look trouble straight in the face, recognizing it for what it is. There are never more than two real choices available to man. On the one hand, despair, which leads to eternal destruction, and on the other, faith, which is the road to salvation. The preacher, however, has a dual role. He always stands in the paradox of two relationships, for he is both priest and prophet. He ministers to men who live in a real world where God works through human instruments holy enough, humble enough, and willing enough to understand His ways and to be used by Him. In this sense, he is a *priest* to the congregation, for he is one of them, and is identified with them in their problems. His function as a *prophet* is to point out to men the way of their salvation, as well as to convict them of their sins. As a prophet proclaiming God's judgment, he stands above them and apart from their situations.

Isaiah was both prophet and priest in the sense that I speak of. This is clearly seen in chapters twenty-four and fifty-four, and in the magnificent fortieth chapter, where,   mingling melancholy with eternal hope and salvation, he writes of earth's crumbling and God's mercy and salvation. Isaiah saw history falling to pieces before his eyes, but he looked beyond history with eyes of faith and proclaimed the ultimate majesty and power of the eternal God.

It is our task as ministers of the word of God to make plain that the divine order is beyond the order of history. Paradoxically, we know that we cannot escape our finite state, whether in life or death; yet when we try to live by the revealed law of God, we transcend our existence by participating in the infinite, holy and eternal power of God. There are sometimes situations for which we need a Jeremiah to thunder the prophecies of inescapable doom, but there are always moments for an Isaiah to recall us from exile.

In the prophetic role, it is the preacher's task to help make the society and the church aware of a message adequate to the needs of the times—with a power and a force which can survive even when the foundations crumble. Many aspects of modern civilization—our wars, our fears, our economic injustices, our colonialism, our prejudices—cannot, and do not deserve to be saved. Some things about our civilization, when judged by the religion of Jesus, must be changed or must die. Civilization needs to be cleansed, redeemed, and regenerated at a deep level, so that it may rise to a great height. To do this, men of faith and love will have to make sacrifices. They may sometimes have to suffer. There is no redemption without pain, suffering, and penitence.

There are, of course, values in our civilization which will and ought to survive because they are at the center of truth. But the difficulty is that we have so identified all of our cultural, economic, and political formulas with the essential truths of Christianity that we hesitate to purge any of them. Willingness to surrender is the most terrifying fact men have to face in their endeavor to achieve world peace, better race relations, or a transfiguration of world order. Even Christianity has to be revitalized and redeemed from social barnacles which encrust its body, and this can only be done by deep humility, profound soul-searching, and religious renewal among its clergy and its laity. Reformation is not a static, one-period event lost in time, mellowed with age, and hallowed with reverence. Reformation is a living need for creative growth and development. Reformation was perhaps never more urgently needed than it is today; certainly it is needed as much now as it was in the sixteenth century.

To confuse the church as an end, rather than as a means to the glory of God transcendent above, is as bad as the fallacy of confusing the means by which we live with the ends for which we live. Any means—religious, practical, or scientific—which comes to be regarded as an indispensable end, will ultimately destroy the very ground of our existence. Means must always be subordinate to ends. One of the greatest fallacies and source of trouble in our Western culture is the confusion of means and ends and the consequent subordination of ends to means. Walter Horton has pointed out, "There is no surer sign of decay than the exaggerated importance attached to these peripheral elements in our Western social system."

The dual role of the preacher is not an easy one. Dr. Paul Tillich poignantly describes the difficulty of this dual role when he says of the prophet Isaiah:

> He knew two orders of being: the human, political, historical order; and the divine, eternal order. Because Isaiah knew these two orders, he could speak as he did, moving continually between the depth of human nothingness and the great height of divine creativity . . . In speaking of them we speak of ourselves, because we belong to both of them in every moment of our lives and history.[1]

The ministry of the preacher must be to men and women as and where they are. Men live, work, love, create, worship, and die amid a cultural, political, social, and economic environment which they help make, and which in turn conditions and molds them. Their spiritual anchors are shifted by "every stormy wind that blows and every swelling tide of woes."

The mores of our existence are often in conflict with the religion we propose. The temptation to compromise unnecessarily and unduly is always present. The minister, however, must turn from the human order to the divine order, like Isaiah, in order to judge righteously. He has the delicate task of working within the human order where men dwell, for men can work out protocols, policies, and programs of cooperative existence only through the instruments and means at their disposal. Thus his task is incredibly difficult—to help men work through the torments of practical and human institutions, while at the same time helping them to measure their institutions and their lives by the judgment of God! Gospel insight is the way to help man view himself as a citizen of *this* world in the light of "his citizenship in the Kingdom."

The hour calls for an adventurous faith in the ultimate victory of righteousness over evil, justice over tyranny, and the might and love of God over the forces of irreligion. Every age has its own time of trouble and crisis in one form or another. Some are more earth-shaking than others, but no time in the history of the world has seen more extensive disaster and drunk more bitter dregs of sorrow than ours. The whole world is involved in the crisis of Western civilization, because the West has penetrated every corner of the globe in one or more aspects of its culture, economics, politics, or religion. The mechanical genius of the West has brought the ends of the earth almost within a day's journey. No spot, therefore, is safe from aggression.

Civilizations have risen and fallen before, some never to rise again, and others to recreate themselves in a new spirit. Walter Horton bids us look to the past for evidence of the power of religion to save, redeem, and recreate in advanced civilizations as it had done in primitive cultures. He holds to the thesis that religions have done this in the past in Asia, the Middle East and Europe—provided religion exhibited the power to renew its active influence through self-criticism and reform. He presents a wealth of evidence to support his thesis in *Can Christianity Save Civilization*. It is his foremost premise that we realize at once that "although we seem at times helpless, we are never hopeless if our trust and faith are securely anchored in eternal concepts beyond our institutions and our time."

One of the important tasks for the preacher is to call for a firm, adventurous faith which will move forward unafraid in the darkest hour of trial "when all around gives way." The average Christian will launch out upon a daring and creative offensive if leaders of faith, wisdom, and courage will spur him on.

I once spoke to a group of young white Southerners in Texas who were discouraged about their future, the nation's future, and the world's future. They saw no reason for working for a better world when every effort seemed to no avail. They could see little sense in completing their education since most of them were soon to be called to the army; they talked of postponing their life's work and their marriages. Some of them, they knew, would die in Korea in a war that was not even called a war. They were also deeply troubled by the fact that only with great difficulty had they obtained the permission of their Christian elders to invite me, a Negro, to be their leader.

I saw that my job was cut out for me. I had to help them see that "beyond the veil of wrath and tears where looms but the horror of the shade" were the resources of God's power which could revitalize the latent power within themselves. I had to make them sure that once they caught hold of it they were no longer helpless. For, like St. Paul, they could "do all things through Christ."

I spoke to these young men about Isaiah and his call; I used it to show them the necessity of self-examination and contrite preparation for the tasks ahead in time of trouble and change. I called to their attention my own example of willingness to be expendable to prejudice by coming to Texas and sharing God's love through suffering with them.

And then I offered them a first step—the job of helping me secure books for African students who wanted the light of knowledge and who desired to inherit the same world of security, justice, freedom, and peace as our students.

They rose at once to the opportunity. They not only collected over forty thousand books, not only raised sufficient funds to ship the volumes to New York, but they also amassed nearly five thousand dollars, sufficient funds to send a librarian out to Africa. From that beginning, a bridge of over two hundred thousand volumes of books has been built. It is a bridge of light and hope linking a group of young Texans with thousands of other young people in awakening Africa—inspiring them with this witness of faith.

This adventure in trust and faith seems pitifully small and almost irrelevant to some adults to whom I tell the story. It is, they seem to say, too little an effort; too far removed; it can't possibly be of sufficient weight to help tilt the gigantic scales of an international struggle. "It's like trying to push a loaded coal car off a railroad siding with a feather," some of them lamented. But in the awakening continent of Africa, where the battle for the souls and minds of men is being joined, its effect was far more significant than any of us could possibly have dreamed.

I saw the power of the trust and faith of those students demonstrated all over Africa. I heard it in the throb of the talking drums as I entered a village way back in the bush, miles beyond the last telephone pole and rail-head: "The man who aroused the students of his country to love us with books has come." I heard it at least a hundred times.

Then there was the old, old woman in Nigeria who offered me an egg—her only possession!—and who through an interpreter told me at a reception in my honor, given by ten thousand people, "I can't read. I have no children who can read, but somebody has children who can read, and many more will read one day. I give you all I have with love and thanks for the young of your land who have sent us good things that are right and wise."

Little though she knew it, this old woman spoke for thousands. Not long after my return to the United States the Prime Minister of Eastern Nigeria—the Honorable Nnamdi Azikiwe—wrote to tell me of his people's gratitude. Then he went on to say that because of the books, his government had been inspired to establish a National Library Board.

A great many Christians today are as anxious and as fearful as were these Southern lads—*and just as able, just as ready to share in an adventure of faith!* The providence of God in the face of demoniac forces loose in the world may at times seem utterly unbelievable, impractical, if not altogether impossible. Even the idea of God seems implausible to many. The realities of the world appear to negate righteousness and divine purpose so thoroughly that men merely cling to belief in God as a hope against the absence of hope. For many, life has ceased to have meaning, and history has no future.

The preacher's answer to such pessimism is that these persons have ceased to trust God's ultimate love and power, and have refused to recognize their own involvement in, and responsibility for, the sins of the social order. Actually, their fears are but an extension and a rationalization of the pride which refuses to accept the condemnation of God for failures. Until we can accept the wrath of God's judgment, we can never understand His providence.

This demands an adventuring faith. God's providence is not proved by a state of continual peace, goodness, and happiness permeating our situation in life without reference to our belief or disbelief, our failures or our successes. Rather, it is proved by the fact that in every condition of life, the goodness of God cannot be destroyed by the satanic forces of the world, or by our refusal to face our guilt. Providence gives us the light to see the way, and the freedom to choose it—but we must choose. When we choose rightly, the providence of God provides that nothing can separate us from the love of God which is in Christ Jesus. This is not a state of predestined planning so that men do not suffer, but a transcendency of the human being over suffering as he ventures with God. Our nation needs this new adventure because it seems to want salvation and redemption without a cross.

Faith in God, faith in the future, faith in God's children, makes us see that we are never helpless so long as we are engaged in working "together for good to them that love God." This is neither a general faith, nor a false faith. Men can also die for a false faith. Men die today for Communism, and they died yesterday for Nazism. Commitment can be given to lower ways of life as easily, if not more so, than to God's way of love. Men do it every day. A general faith is too nebulous.

The choice today is not between faith and no faith, but between competing faiths. The failure to understand this relatively simple problem has led Americans to waste precious time and energy, and to make naive and sometimes ridiculous moves in the battle against Communism. The faith for this hour must be a definite and specific faith with transcendental anchors. It is faith, not in our transitory institutions, but in the eternal ideals for which they were created; faith in a divinity we can worship in spirit and in truth;

the faith which both outlives, and, when necessary, outdies all other faiths.

Such a faith costs something—every moral advance has its price tag. Kikuyu Christians in Kenya are paying the supreme price against the Mau Mau, and when the new history of China is written in the future, we will read stories of heroism for the Christian faith which will rival anything in the annals of Christendom.

A faith like this cannot be destroyed. This was the faith of St. Augustine after the collapse of the foundations upon which the Roman empire built the world of its day. It is a faith which our forefathers raised in an ancient folk song when they sang:

> That cause can never be lost or stayed
> Which takes the course of what God has made
> And is not trusting in walls and towers
> But slowly growing from seeds to flowers.

II

No problems resulting from the convolutions of a civilization in travail need more urgent attention from the preacher than those caused by egotism and self—or cultural—deification. One of the deep infirmities of every individual, every group, every race, and every nation is egotism. If egotism fosters illusions of importance and indispensability in moderately successful circumstances, we do not need to stretch our imaginations very far to understand what it has done to Westerners, who have been eminently successful in their mastery over geography, climate, time, space, technology, and nature. The besetting sin of the West is the twin illusions which we hug to ourselves of the ultimate superiority of our whole way of life and the invincibility of our technological genius and scientific power.

Self-glorification and deification always lead to complacency, indifference, self-righteousness, and false presuppositions about the reasons for our success.

Complacency and indifference are more difficult to deal with than overt hatred, hostility, sin, and evil. Hate is but the opposite of love; hostility, the opposite of humility; sin, the opposite of righteousness; and evil, the opposite of goodness. Complacency and indifference are too nebulous to take hold at any point.

Belief and trust in the power at our disposal is an intoxicant which leads to unwarranted illusions of invincibility and omnipotence. The Psalmist knew the dangerous temptation of trusting in force and power when he sang, "Some trust in chariots, and some in horses; but we will remember the name of the Lord our God." (PSALMS 20:7) The gravest danger is the fact that we may come close—that, indeed, we are already dangerously close—to a reliance upon power by itself alone as the way out of our dilemma. Worse: in a moment of crisis, the danger is ever present that we may unleash the power at our disposal in an act of desperation and regret it later. This possibility gives greater alarm to America's allies than most of our citizens realize. They know that there are those among us who sometimes lack good judgment, that we have more than our share of men who love to play the role of God.

The preacher of the gospel of Christ cannot allow himself to be derelict in addressing himself to this perplexing, continually increasing problem. Despite the fact that power concepts are here to stay, the preacher has something to say not only about its use and control, but about a power far greater, far more constructive, and far more enduring than any scientist's combination of molecules. Moreover, the preacher's supreme task is relating men to the right and wise stewardship of the tremendous forces at their disposal. This part of his task is greater than ever because it is most difficult to curb the tendency toward pride and arrogance, and to develop a spirit of humility and a sense of interdependence, when so much of this world's goods are in our hands, and when we, with the possible exception of the Soviets, have overwhelming stockpiles of atomic and hydrogen weapons, and the means and wealth to make so many more.

The West describes power in terms of physical force: hydrogen and atomic bombs, guided missiles and supersonic jet planes, vast quantities of machines and tools of industry, tremendous stores of wealth and almost unlimited capital. This is the power we are proud of and upon which we confidently rely. Yet nearly half the world's population have changed their form of government, created a new hope for a brighter and more secure future, and thrown off the yoke of oppression without reference to a single element of power as we know it. Millions more are in the process of doing the same thing, and they will succeed sooner or later. Gandhi had only a spinning wheel and some invincible ideas of faith, freedom, peace, and human dignity, but he and his followers threw the British out of India. Others like him—without guns, ships, planes, money and great industries—have done the same in other areas of Asia and Africa. It was this same spiritual power which our forefathers had in the early days of our country; it made us a great nation. And people—they are elements of power far greater and far more resourceful than money, tools, ships, and guns.

Spiritual power is as valid as ever, for it is the force of redemption and salvation in every human situation. History amply records the disasters of all the Napoleons, Hitlers, and Stalins—all those who, like the Assyrians, had the weight of overwhelming physical superiority on their side. Force and power are not inevitable guarantees of victory; rather they lead to gross miscalculations of strength in the face of the superior moral and spiritual forces of the universe. To rely upon power because of a lagging faith in the righteous will and justice of God is to deny that this is God's world, that He made it, and saw that it was good despite its conflicts, that He rules it, despite the fact that many have tried to usurp His role, and that He is still in it, redeeming it because He loves it and its people.

Physical force and power are not the last words. God's will, love, justice, and redemption are the last word. "Not by might, but by my spirit, saith the Lord." There can be no proper horizontal relationship between man and man until it is motivated by a higher, perpendicular relationship between God and man.

The greatest menace to the West is not Communism, but the West itself, deluded by false pretense and its effort to compromise in its relations to God. This compromise, within, can be more destructive in the long run, than any forces from without. Com-

munism can be defeated. Indeed, it will defeat itself, for it carries
within itself the seeds of its own destruction, since it does not
square with the pre-established harmony of God's laws of love
and destiny. But we need to overcome that fatuous passivity toward the present which springs from an infatuation with past glory
and greatness, and is, indeed, the sin of self-importance and of
idolatry. We must cease our glorification of human achievement,
our "blind worship of the creature instead of the Creator." Nothing so vitiates and undermines the foundations of a social order
as the idolization of a glorious past. Toynbee writes wisely when
he says:

> It may take the form of an idolization of the idolater's
> own personality or society in some ephemeral phase of
> a never ceasing movement through challenge, which
> is the essence of being alive; or it may take the limited
> form of some idolization of some particular institution or
> technique which once stood the idolater in good stead.[2]

Under such circumstances, we may become so enamoured of
ourselves and our institutions that we think the enemies of our
culture, nation, or civilization are also the enemies of God. This is
not necessarily so, although sometimes they are. As often, however, they are the agents of God. Cyrus, the founder of the Per-
sian empire, was an enemy of Israel, but not an enemy of God.
Cyrus was in the service of God, although he perhaps did not
know that he was carrying out God's purpose.

The God we all must follow is not a God which is the creation
of our own image, one who loves us above all others, one who
hates the Communists because we hate them. Yet religious life
comes pretty close to that in our country when we cannot see
distinction between the necessity of hating Communism, and, at
the same time, loving the Communists. A God whom we thus
create and possess cannot save us or our civilization, for he is no
longer God with the majesty and power to transform personal
and historical life. We cannot possess God. He possesses us.

We were so sure of our own greatness, for example, when we

talked about the white man's burden that we failed to recognize the latent potentialities in other human beings, and they at length rose to overtake us. We have now changed the expression to "underdeveloped peoples," but the condescending terms and patronizing methods we often use fool neither God nor the people of underdeveloped areas.

Although Christianity's contact with the peoples of Asia and Africa in the past was often corrupted by the colonialism, Western technology, capital, and military conquest with which it was associated, nevertheless it was Christianity's spiritual witnessing which in the end made the most lasting, positive, and constructive impact upon the people and their cultures. When all else has been crushed, thrust aside, and crumbled, Christianity in one form or another has survived. It has outlasted every tyrant, outlived every persecution, and grown strong with every indignity it has suffered. It is often changed in the process, and its adherents always have to bear an almost intolerable amount of suffering, but it stands. Despite the great recrudescence of Eastern religions, there is hope for missions. Not perhaps as we know the missionary enterprise of the past, but certainly there is hope for that essence of missions which is inherent in the spiritual ideas of the Kingdom of God. Missions never placed their ultimate reliance on material power, but in forces of the spirit.

There will be grave difficulties ahead, and a time may come when we cannot send missionaries into many areas of the world, but the Church will survive, and the Kingdom will come "whate'er betide!" If European and American missionaries are asked out of mission lands, and the nationals who accepted their faith are persecuted, this will not mean that the cause is lost. It is a fallacious theology which makes escape from suffering or unmitigated success the criteria for faith in the ultimate triumph of our God and His Church. As a matter of fact, the weight of empirical evidence is on the side of the fact that the good constantly suffer, and that good does not win out in every particular situation. God Himself has taken the initiative to demonstrate through Jesus Christ that the good is often crucified. But He has also demonstrated that in the long last, the good which was pillared, defeated, and even crucified, overcomes and is finally triumphant.

Missions of the future need not work out according to our well-conceived and skillfully-organized plans. And it may well be that the indigenous Christian leadership in which Western Christian leaders have put too little trust and have been so slow to bring into full partnership and responsibility, will spread the Kingdom farther and faster in the future. It is reasonable to suggest that the supreme task of missions in a day of crumbling foundations is to put the best tools in the hands of indigenous Christian leaders in mission lands, put the best education at their disposal, and give them our greatest support with faith that God will accomplish greater results through them than we ever dreamed were possible. Western missionary leaders have often made the same mistake of Western political, economic, and cultural leaders who have misled the converts into feeling that they need us but we do not need them. The fact is we need the world more than it needs us. The greater part of mankind is outside the physical boundaries of the West.

What they will achieve will not be a form of practical Christian expression and organization as we have developed it in the West. And there is no earthly or heavenly reason why it should be an adaptation of Western patterns in every detail. The universality of the gospel is seen better in its diversity than in a static imposition of the cultural expression with which it is of necessity overlaid. And our brothers who lead the younger churches will make many mistakes, just as all of us have erred in both our past and present history. The Kingdom does not depend upon the strategy and techniques developed in the missionary headquarters any more that it does upon the expansion of democracy or the survival of the United States. This is not to imply that the mission leaders are neither necessary nor important, nor that we do not need organization, strategy, planning, and machinery, nor that the democratic way of life is not conducive to the work of the Kingdom. But it is to say that we need a longer perspective, and that the Kingdom cannot be measured in terms of worldly success and progress.

There can be no doubt about the fact that millions in mission lands may not have accepted the gospel of Jesus, but they *have* been more powerfully influenced and changed by it than many of them recognize. Thousands readily admit to the power of the gospel even if they do not embrace it. Millions with disillusioned minds and disappointed hearts are receptive to a gospel of spiritual power and resource which will lift them above the mire of tragedy. And Christianity is that gospel, with the ultimate and triumphant power to rescue them and us.

The Christian gospel is not Utopian and does not envision a perfect world order where there are no problems, no heartaches, no pain, no suffering, no discipline, no necessity to labor indefatigably against tremendous odds to overcome evil. Its mission to men is within time, within history, within geography, and within human situations. It looks toward world order beyond and above, which helps to improve this world by holding a higher judgment always before them. The Christian gospel is not sentimental escapism—nor is it defeatism. It faces the hard realities of historical limitations. Its peculiar genius is to point men to a conceivably better world than they already have, by the recognition that all human adjustments and social achievements are made by compromise, and are therefore tentative and subject to continual reform, revision, and improvement. Jesus dealt with these hard realities when he prayed, "I pray not that Thou should take them out of the world, but that Thou shouldest keep them from evil. . . . As Thou has sent me into the world, even so have I also sent them into the world." (St. John 17:15,18) It is a valid Christian insight that all systems of government, economics and social culture are made by man and operated for man, and that although one system may be immeasurably preferable to other systems, all are nevertheless under the judgment of God. The Christian gospel does not offer a blueprint for the future, but it offers the high and eternal goals which continually call us to the ultimate possibilities as sons of God. It calls us to a confrontation of our situation in the light of the Christian insight that God does not leave us to stand alone.

III

No foundations ever crumbled more completely than those of the Negro slave, and no people ever saw better the ultimate vindication of their faith and hope. The old Negro preacher, as James Welden Johnson wrote in *God's Trombones*, has not yet been given the niche in which he properly belongs:

> He has been portrayed only as a semi-comic figure. He had, it is true, his comic aspects, but on the whole he was an important figure, and at the bottom a vital factor... He was the first shepherd of his bewildered flock. His powers for good or ill were very great. It was the old-time preacher who for generations was the mainspring of hope for the Negro in America.[3]

And it was this same uneducated and unordained prophet-priest who inspired the spirituals, for he saw through the pride and pretensions of men to the ultimate power of God.

Suddenly cut off from the moorings of his native culture, transported as chattel into a strange land with a strange language, scattered without regard to his family ties, sold on the auction block with no more regard than the auctioneer would give to cattle, beaten with the whip by men who professed the love of God and the brotherhood of man, he nevertheless lifted his soul above his trial and his voice above the contradiction and tumult to give America in the spiritual its most beautiful artistic achievement.

These songs of faith are the expression of his faith—a contemporary evidence that God never leaves himself without a witness. Through the spirituals he saw hope rising out of despair and loneliness. In the agony of his solitude when all his temporary foundations gave way, he found in the deeper introspection of religion that "trouble doesn't last always." He marched out to meet the promise of God which he understood in his heart but could only express clearly in a song like, "Go Down, Moses, way down in Egypt land and tell old Pharoah to let my people go." Surely there is no grander and truer theme in all history.

The spirituals are magnificent songs of faith which express all the cardinal virtues of Christianity—love, forbearance, patience, humility, faith, courage and hope. The slave was not impelled by hatred and he did not rail against God. It is remarkable that he had the insight to separate the eternal values of religion from the husks which were offered him. The apparent escapism, naivete, and emotionalism of the language in which the spirituals were cast have never been an adequate measure of their depth of religious insight . . . an insight always more profoundly social, political, and theological than most of us have understood.

The spirituals preach the adventure of Christianity.

Christianity is not an illusion. It is real, and its faith and methods have been proved in fire and famine, by persecution and prison, by the sword and the stake, by heroism and humility, by slave and by king, by the rich and the poor, through the most excruciating agony. It has survived the time and change of every human institution in which men have found themselves. It rose above the ruins of Imperial Rome; it survived the dark ages and ushered in the enlightenment. It can steady our shaking foundations and build stronger and more enduring ones when those that ought to die have crumbled into dust.

> We are troubled on every side, yet
> not distressed; we are perplexed,
> but not in despair;
>
> Persecuted, but not forsaken; cast
> down, but not destroyed;
>
> For our light affliction, which is
> but for a moment, worketh for us a far
> more exceeding and eternal weight of
> glory;
>
> While we look not at the things
> which are seen, but at the things
> which are not seen: for the things
> which are seen are temporal; but the
> things which are not seen are eternal.
>
> II CORINTHIANS 4:8, 9, 17, 18

NOTES

NOTES

CHAPTER ONE, THE PREACHER UNDER JUDGMENT

1—"Untrained Negro Clergy," by Ralph A. Felton, Christian Century, February 2, 1955.

2—Bertrand Russell, *Human Society in Ethics and Politics,* (Simon & Schuster, Inc., 630 Fifth Avenue, New York 20, N.Y.)

3—Charles Lindbergh, *Of Flight and Life* (Charles Scribner's Sons. 597 Fifth Avenue, New York, 17, N.Y.)

4—Elton Trueblood, *The Predica-ment of Modern Man* (Harper & Brothers, 49 East 33rd Street, New York 16, N.Y.)

5—James Robinson, *Road Without Turning* (Farrar, Straus & Cudahy, Inc., 101 Fifth Avenue, New York 3, N.Y.)

6—Reinhold Niebuhr, Editor, *This Ministry* (Charles Scribner's Sons, 597 Fifth Avenue, New York 17, N.Y.)

CHAPTER TWO, THE FELLOWSHIP OF CONFESSION

1—Charles Kean, *Making Sense Out of Life* (Westminster Press, Witherspoon Building, Philadelphia 7, Pa.)

2—Halford Luccock, *Communicating the Gospel* (Harper & Brothers, 49 East 33rd Street, New York 16, N.Y.)

3—Anne Morrow Lindbergh, *Gift from the Sea* (Pantheon Books, Inc., 333 Sixth Avenue, New York 14, N.Y.)

4—Gerald Kennedy, *With Singleness of Heart* (Harper & Brothers, 49 East 33rd Street, New York 16, N.Y.)

5—Leslie Weatherhead, *The Signif-icance of Silence* (Abingdon Press, 810 Broadway, Nashville 2, Tenn.)

6—*opus cit.*

7—Seward Hiltner, *Pastoral Counseling* (Abingdon Press, 810 Broadway, Nashville 2, Tenn.)

8—Karl Stern, *The Third Revolution* (Harcourt, Brace & Company, 383 Madison Avenue, New York 17, N.Y.)

9—The Annual Directory of Pastoral Psychology magazine, published in January of each year, contains a complete list of training centers conducted by these two organizations throughout the country.

10—Joshua Loth Liebman, *Peace of*

Mind (Simon & Schuster, Inc. 630 Fifth Avenue, New York 20, N.Y.)

11—Frances G. Wickes, *The Inner*

Life of Man (Henry Holt & Company, Inc., 383 Madison Avenue, New York 17, N.Y.)

CHAPTER THREE, PREACHING TO MEN OR MORTAR

1—Murray H. Leiffer, *The Effective City Church* (Abingdon Press, 810 Broadway, Nashville 2, Tenn.)

2—"Shine, Perishing Republic," in *Roan Stallion*, by Robinson Jeffers (Boni & Liveright.)

3—Dr. Barry delivered this lecture at Holiday Hills, New York, October 27, 1954; it later was published as "Mortar and Mortals," in *The City Church*, November-December, 1954.

4—Henry Sloane Coffin, *What to*

Preach (Harper & Brothers, 49 East 33rd Street, New York 16, N.Y.)

5—"Going Down This Street, Lord," by William Harlan Hale, *The Reporter*, January 13, 1955.

6—From the January, 1955, issue of *Social Progress*, published by the Department of Social Education and Action of the Board of Christian Education, Presbyterian Church in the U.S.A.

CHAPTER FOUR, CRUMBLING FOUNDATIONS

1—Paul Tillich, *Shaking of the Foundations* (Charles Scribner's Sons, 597 Fifth Avenue, New York 17, N.Y.)

2—*opus cit.*

3—Charles Kean, *Christianity and the Cultural Crisis* (Association

Press, 291 Broadway, New York 7, N.Y.)

4—Walter Horton, *Can Christianity Save Civilization* (Harper & Brothers, 49 East 33rd Street, New York 16, N.Y.)

CHAPTER FIVE, PREACHING TO PRESERVE A NATION

1—*opus cit.*

2—William Ernest Hocking, *What Man Can Make of Man* (Harper & Brothers, 49 East 33rd Street, New York 16, N.Y.)

3—Walter Lippman, *The Public Philosophy* (Little, Brown &

Company, 34 Beacon Street, Boston 6, Mass.)

4—Mr. MacLeish gave this address on the Fortieth Anniversary of the Anti-Defamation League, November 21, 1953.

CHAPTER SIX, THE INCLUSIVENESS OF THE WORD MADE FLESH

1—Paul Scherer, *The Plight of Freedom* (Harper & Brothers, 49

East 33rd Street, New York 16, N.Y.)

CHAPTER SEVEN, HOPE WITHOUT DESPAIR

1—*opus cit.*

2—Arnold Toynbee, *The World and the West* (Oxford University Press, 114 Fifth Avenue, New York 11, N.Y.)

3—James Weldon Johnson, *God's Trombones* (Viking Press, Inc., 18 East 48th Street, New York 17, N.Y.)